Five Pillars

Of

The Apostolic

Towards a Mature Church

Authored by
Dr. Michael Scantlebury

Foreword by
Walter Boston, Jr.

Capitalization:

Dr. Scantlebury has taken *author's prerogative* in capitalizing certain words that are not usually capitalized according to standard grammatical practice. The references to apostles and purity are capitalized and bolded many times to give greater emphasis to the main theme of this book. Also, please note that the name satan and related names are not capitalized as we choose not to acknowledge him, even to the point of disregarding standard grammatical practice.

All scripture quotations, unless otherwise indicated, are taken from the New King James Version. Copyright © 1982 by Thomas Nelson, Inc. Used by permission. All rights reserved.

Hebrew and Greek definitions are taken from James Strong, *Strong's Exhaustive Concordance of the Bible* (Peabody, MA: Hendrickson Publishers, n.d.).

FIVE PILLARS OF THE APOSTOLIC
ISBN 1-894928-10-5
© Copyright 2000 by Michael Scantlebury

Printed by: Word Alive Press Inc.

Editorial Consultant: Amrita Bastians

Cover Design by:
The Visual Limited – www.the-visual.com

Dedication

I first dedicate this book to the Apostle and High Priest of my confession, Christ Jesus. I am truly grateful to Him for granting me the Grace to write this book. More specifically it is dedicated to my wife Sandra for her tireless support and commitment to God's purpose and to our children Candice, Rachel and Samuel who have been standing with me in the ministry. They understood as I spent countless hours writing this book.

In Appreciation

To Dr. Noel Woodroffe of Elijah Centre, Trinidad West Indies for the wisdom and revelation the Lord imparted into my life through him. To the family of believers at Dominion-Life International Ministries (formerly Kingdom Restoration Centre); who gave me the opportunity to minister much of what is in this book as it became clear to me. I also acknowledge Kelvin Thomas and The Visual Limited who designed the cover for the book; Pastor Edward and Pamela Chu for their tremendous support and encouragement, and Amrita Bastians, Sheldon Cyrus and Paulette Affoon for their unselfish assistance in proof reading the manuscripts.

Endorsements For
Five Pillars of the Apostolic

The body of Christ truly is reaching unprecedented levels of power, revelation, and effectiveness. Michael Scantlebury is a keen observer of this historic transition and the key role that apostles are playing in it. Five Pillars of the Apostolic has my recommendation.

C. Peter Wagner, Chancellor
Wagner Leadership Institute

The 21st century has exploded in Apostolic revelation and understanding. It has always been in the bible but very little has been written or understood about this truth. It is my joy to read the original manuscript of *Five Pillars of the Apostolic*.

As I read it, I thought about how important this is in the new millennium. With clarity and simplicity, *Five Pillars* of *the Apostolic* has accurately and clearly unfolded the gift, the gifting, the ministry and the ultimate end results.

After 51 years of Apostolic ministry in thirty-five nations of the world, I have seen a great hunger and need for an understanding of Apostles and Apostolic functions.

God is restoring the Church, firstly through the Apostles. The Apostles have always been ignored in teachings and in books of doctrine, as if they no longer exist. There are many who are afraid of the title and the implications of whether or not Apostles are alive and well today.

I highly recommend this book not only to church leaders but to lay-people everywhere. It will be very informative and helpful in bringing the church to the next level. I thank God for this book by Dr. Scantlebury. *It's a book whose time has come.*

Apostle Emanuele Cannistraci
Apostolic Leader of Apostolic Missions International
San Jose, California, USA

Michael Scantlebury's book, *The Five-Pillars of the Apostolic*, seeks to find a biblical, a balanced, and a logical approach to explaining the ministry of today's apostles. It is a timely expression since so much of what is being said and written today about apostles and apostolic ministry lacks strong biblical basis and is often extreme and contradictory. This book provides an excellent tool for the Church to measure apostolic claims by the yardstick of the author's five-pillars of apostolic grace. Additionally, this book sets the standards appropriately high for those who have the high-calling of apostle. Best of all, Elder Scantlebury's book is Christ-centered in its approach, revealing Jesus Christ as the real answer to each fundamental and eternal question rather than apostles in themselves. Those called, as apostles ought to keep this book nearby to remind them to pray regularly that the five-pillars of the apostolic would be set strongly into their lives and that they might clearly reveal Christ, the Apostle, in humble service.

Dr. Roger W. Sapp
All Nations Ministries
Southlake, Texas, USA

Rooted firmly in biblical teachings this book is a "must" for all leaders who desire to keep their Churches on the cutting edge - in these exciting times in the history of the Church. Profound and powerful, *Five Pillars of the Apostolic* epitomizes the author's prophetic insight and instead of a fragmented view of the Church you could now see the whole picture. This book could be the lever that could change your Church.

Pastor Ajith Abeyratne
Senior Pastor, Calvary Church
Mirihana, Sri Lanka

God is restoring the foundational ministry of the Apostle back to the body of Christ in these last days, and a powerful and militant church is rising in the earth. As God's anointing is released and evidenced through the Apostolic ministry, there will be great debate over the veracity of this calling. Michael's book on the Apostolic presents a sound Biblical perspective. "*The Five Pillars of the Apostolic*" reveals fresh insight into this emerging role in the Church of the new millennia.

Edward D. Chu
Senior Pastor of Christian Life Centre
Vancouver, BC, Canada

I strongly recommend *Five Pillars of the Apostolic* to every Christian who seriously desires to be grounded and established in "present truth." The revelation truths poured forth into this book are biblical, Holy Spirit directed and it could most definitely be a source from which to pick up biblical methods for an effective and supernatural ministry.

In these days, believers cannot be content with only attending church services, but we must seek to learn the wisdom from the sons of Issachar, in order to discern the times we live in. Let us take careful note of the word of God, which cautions us that His people perish for a lack of knowledge. God is doing something dramatic and specific in our day and this book imparts powerful insights that help to understand more clearly what the Holy Spirit is doing in the global Church.

Sergei Atchkassov
President, Breakthrough Ministries
Moscow, Russia

Contents

Foreword   11

Introduction   13

Chapter One: An Overview of Things   17
Upward Climb of The Church   17
Accuracy – A Divine Requirement   18
Purity and Holiness   19
The Ministry of Christ   21
God's Timetable   23
Why The Need For Restoration   24
Understanding God's Restorative Process   27
Apostolic Reference In Scriptures   30
The Third-Day Church   33

Chapter Two: Apostolic Reference and Definition   39
Apostolic Commissioning and Sending   39
The First Principle   43
The Holy Spirit's Intent   44
The Man-Child Anointing   50

Chapter Three: Pillar One   53
Spirit of Wisdom   53
The Zerubbabel Example   56
The Moses Example   60
The Daniel Example   61
Paul's Example   70

Chapter Four: Pillar Two   73
Fathering   73
Elijah and Elisha   75
Qualities of True Fathers   84
True Apostolic Fathers vs. Traditional Religious Leaders   86
The Heart Cry of True Apostles   96

Chapter Five: Pillar Three 101
Government and Authority 101
The Threshing Floor of Ornan the Jebusite 108
Issues of the Contents of the Ark 109

Chapter Six: Pillar Four 115
Wealth 115
The Wealth Transfer 118
Kingdom Business 119
Babylon will be judged 125

Chapter Seven: Pillar Five 131
Miracles, Signs and Wonders 131
Meaning and Origin of Miracles 134
An Interesting Event 137

Chapter Eight: The Apostles and Church Unity 143
Networking 152
Purity, Part of the Process Towards a United Church 154

Appendix 157
Questions and Answers 157

Other Titles By The Author

Foreword

Discerning seasons and times is such an important task in the day that we live. If, as the body of the LORD we fail to do so, we will fail in expressing the heart of Father God. Being a pupil of biblical studies and church history for twenty-four years, I am fully cognizant of the real need to be relevant and accurate, in the proclamation of truth.

These days are filled with a myriad of religious expressions that leave masses of spiritual seekers in a haven of confusion. For some, it is the lack of knowledge, for others, it is the practice of that which is heathen, while for others, it is the entrapment of old traditions that annul the power of the gospel. I believe we are swiftly approaching a time when we must have a clear understanding of what is happening, as it relates to kingdom building. The bottom line is that where the church was in history, it no longer is. Where we are - we must not remain, and as for the future, we must not only *know* the mind of Christ, but we must exercise it.

If you were to take a journey through the archives of biblical history scholars, it would reveal that with each period of time there was an emphasis. No matter whom the Holy Spirit chose to express Himself through, there would usually be a predominant theme. Upon that great truth, would usher the plan of God into a greater hour. Hereunto have we come upon this hour, *The Greatest Hour Of The Church!*

Five Pillars of the Apostolic, (Towards a Mature Church) is a powerfully wealthy masterpiece that meticulously speaks to today, with balance. It is a culmination of *definitions, history,* and *revelation* that will introduce any serious minded individual to how the *Lord* is using His church *Now.* It is evident; that through much study, and time alone with Jesus, Elder

Scantlebury skilfully expounds upon subjects that will undoubtedly be the pillars of the twenty first-century Church. As I read this book, in many instances I saw truths for the first time, while simultaneously I was able to grab a hold of nuggets and build messages. This great work is a gold mine with much hidden treasure, and would easily become an exceptional resource for any student of the scripture.

The days ahead shall introduce us to the best of good and bad times. To execute the purpose of God and to resolutely advance forward, we will need to possess keys that reveal to us: purpose and destiny. This book is one such key. It unlocks a treasure chest and places at your disposal, truths that will change your life and ministry, clearly enabling you to define your service in the Kingdom.

Jesus in Matthew 16:18 tells us that, "*I will put together my church, a church so expansive with energy that not even the gates of hell will be able to keep it out.*" (The Message) I can say with confidence, that this is the hour He is raising up *Preachers* (Five-fold ministry gifts), *People* (Christians with readiness of desire), and *Plans* (vision that is from the heart of God), that will bring the church to the forefront, in *Majesty*! He is building with grace gifts such as the likes of Elder Scantlebury, who with conviction, principles and practices are leading the way.

Someone once said, "*Minds are like parachutes; they work best when they are open.*" Take a journey into the Five Pillars of the Apostolic and prepare yourself to receive some great inspiration and enlightenment. Thanks Michael, for such a timely piece of revelation. May God cause it to fall into the hands of a people that will impact the whole earth!

Walter Boston, Jr.
Founder and Apostolic Team Leader - C.A.U.S.E. International
Founder and President of Walter Boston Jr. Ministries
Senior Elder, City of Praise, Ahoskie NC, USA

Five Pillars of the Apostolic

Towards a Mature Church

Introduction

It has become very evident that a new day has dawned in the earth, as the Lord restores the foundational ministry of the Apostle back to His Church. And in the next few chapters of this book I will set out to give some definition to what God is saying and doing in the earth today. Peter encourages us by the Holy Spirit to be established in "present truth".

Present Truth is the terminology that was used by the Apostle Peter to describe the revelation of Jesus Christ at that time. Peter states:

"For this reason I will not be negligent to remind you always of these things, though you know and are established in the *present truth*." 2 Peter 1:12 (Italics added)

In this passage of scripture the Apostle Peter was warning the saints, of the false-teachers and erroneous doctrine that would arise, even though they were very current with what the Lord was speaking at that time.

It is from this premise we coin the term "Present-Truth". During the "dark ages" (the period of time from around the 4th to the 15th century), the Church we read about in the book of Acts had fallen into a state of apostasy. Also during that period of time, the "Five-Fold" ministry gifts as outlined in Ephesians 4:11, had disappeared from within the structure of the visible Church.

"And He Himself *gave some to be Apostles, some Prophets, some Evangelists, and some Pastors and some Teachers.* For the equipping of the saints for the work of the ministry, for the edifying of the body of Christ." (Italics added)

It was not until the early 1500's when a German priest named Martin Luther uncovered a powerful "present truth", "the just shall live by faith," that we saw the start of a major transformation of the Church which, to this day, is still in effect. As time elapses, we are seeing "present truth" after "present truth" being restored to the body of Christ, making the word of God relevant to our time.

There is an awesome, powerful, militant church rising in the earth, as Apostles are being restored to take their place alongside the Prophets, Evangelists, Pastors and Teachers to bring the Church into unity and to a place of maturity for function in the earth. It is indeed a glorious time to be alive and be connected to the purposes of the Lord.

It is my prayer that your life be impacted and changed in

reading the pages of this book the way I was in writing it.

Dr. Michael Scantlebury
Founder and Senior Elder
Dominion-Life International Ministries

Chapter One
An Overview of Things

Upward Climb of the Church

As the Church of Jesus Christ continues the upward climb from the abyss of the "Dark Ages" to its place of pre-determined glory of ruling among the nations, we are experiencing a tremendous unfolding of scriptures, as the Holy Spirit releases revelation upon revelation. One such scripture of major importance is Ephesians 4:11-13.

Although we have come to accept the ministry gifts of Evangelists, Pastors and Teachers, it has not been quite so with those of the Apostle and Prophet. To this end God is raising up Prophets as well as end-time Apostles to bring His people into the "fullness" of their inheritance in Christ. Many Apostles and Prophets have been called to begin "networks and schools" in order for many great Apostolic and Prophetic ministers to be raised up.

These networks and schools are primarily purposed to lead those men and women who are called to the Five-Fold ministry, into the "fullness" of their calling in Christ. Having attained the fullness of their calling, these ministers may then lead all those whom God has called them to minister to, into the fullness of their inheritance in Christ. The end result will see a mighty people produced, who will express the kingdom of God in the earth.

Accuracy - A Divine Requirement

God requires accuracy in all that He calls us to do; therefore we must not proceed with any preconceived notions concerning that which God will do, in this last hour. The revelation God is giving to us through His holy Apostles and Prophets in this final hour, is extremely vital to all those whose hearts are wholly given, and whose desire is to accomplish the will of God for their lives. When each of us begin to walk with the Lord, He begins the process of "renewing our minds" in order that we might "begin" to think as He thinks and see as He sees. In the past, many leaders have abused their positions of authority in the church. Because of this, they have disillusioned untold numbers of the children of God. We perceive that at this very time, God is causing a great transition to take place in the hearts of His people, and He is revealing to them a "leadership" that is trustworthy in the handling of His Word and in the building up of His Church in the earth.

We need to fully understand that when anyone who has been called to be an Apostle, Prophet, Evangelist, Pastor or Teacher, declares a "revelation truth", it is simply the outpouring of God's Spirit of wisdom and revelation.

Please understand that the word, or the action, is not first and foremost a by-product of the vessel (Apostle, Prophet, Evangelist, Pastor or Teacher) being used; but rather, the vessel (Apostle, Prophet, Evangelist, Pastor or Teacher) is simply the container or conduit for the teaching of the Holy Spirit and the necessary administration of God's truth.

For too long we, as the children of God, have (to varying degrees) kept our eyes on "flesh and blood" instead of on Jesus. Because of this, at times we have elevated certain of the leaders (Apostles, Prophets, Evangelists, Pastors or Teachers) that God raised up, thereby allowing us to be held captive by a "spirit of idolatry". This undoubtedly prevents one from receiving the fullness of God's blessing, regardless of the office of the vessel God has sent. However, in this season, God is raising up men and women who are driven (at any personal cost) by this one burning desire; and that is to lead people into the fullness of their inheritance in Christ. This will enable them to enter into the fullness of the ministry that God has called them to! Rather than being entities unto themselves, Five-Fold ministers are simply "forerunners" or "pioneers" in the carrying out of God's "Kingdom-Purpose" in the earth.

Purity and Holiness

Those of us who are called to the Five-Fold ministry for the precious work that the Lord is doing in these last days will only survive if we abide in perfect obedience - both individually and corporately. There must be a return to *"Purity and Holiness"*. It is only in this way that the Church can be strong, both foundationally and structurally. This is also the only way to ensure that satan and his "pharisee spirits" are both exposed and "driven out" from the midst of God's people throughout the earth!

There has been a change in the spiritual climate, and now God has ordained the full release of His holy Apostles and Prophets into the Church and the earth. God has surely begun a most glorious work, and we must position ourselves so that there can be a coming together of the Apostles and Prophets. As we do this, we will be assisting in the establishment of the Five-Fold ministry, to operate at its fullest level.

Please understand that when this happens "all hell will break loose," as this is the thing the devil fears most. For satan knows that once the Five-Fold ministry is fully functional, and the saints are equipped to do the work of the ministry, his kingdom will be destroyed. Hence the reason there is such opposition for the full restoration of Apostles and Prophets. However, there is one thing we must all realize as we press forward in this end-time, and that is: *"If this move is of God, nothing or no one can stop it; therefore, we need not attempt to defend it or what we declare!"*

There has never been a move of God that has taken place without problems, but most of the problems are of an internal nature, surrounding those in leadership. However, I declare to you by the Spirit of the living God that we will see a coming together of His body in this hour, such as we have not seen before.

The word that Jesus spoke *"I will build my Church and the gates of hell will not prevail against it"* is still in effect up to this very day. The knowledge of His glory shall literally fill the earth as the waters cover the sea. In order to accomplish this, as we said before, Christ has distributed ministry gifts, which enable the Church to function as His Body. But the five gifts of Ephesians 4:11 have a special purpose:

The Ministries - Verse 11 - these five ministry gifts are not merely "titles", but ministry functions. There is nothing "elevated" about these gifts (1 Corinthians 4:9-13). They simply have a special purpose.

The Purpose - Verse 12 - "...to prepare God's people for works of service, so that the body of Christ may be built up." These five leadership gifts were not simply given *to do the work* of the ministry, but *to enable God's people to do the work of the ministry.*

The Time Frame - Verse 13 - "...until we all reach unity in the faith and in the knowledge of the Son of God and become mature, attaining to the whole measure of the fullness of Christ." The Five-Fold ministry did not pass away at the end of the first century, but was given until the maturing of the Body in unity, knowledge and expression of Christ's fullness.

The Ministry Of Christ

The Five-Fold ministry gifts are examples of how "grace has been given as Christ apportioned it" (Ephesians 4:7). All ministries are simply the ministry of Christ expressed through the believer by the anointing of the Holy Spirit.

Christ Is Our Apostle
"Therefore, holy brethren, partakers of the heavenly calling, consider *the Apostle* and High Priest of our confession, Christ Jesus." Hebrews 3:1 (Italics added)

Christ Is Our Prophet
"And He said to them, 'What things?' So they said to Him, "The things concerning *Jesus of Nazareth, who was a Prophet* mighty in deed and word before God and all the people." Luke 24:19 (Italics added)

Christ Is Our Evangelist
"And He was handed the book of the Prophet Isaiah. And when He had opened the book, He found the place where it was written: The Spirit of the Lord is upon Me,

Because He has anointed Me *To preach the gospel* to the poor; He has sent Me to heal the brokenhearted, To proclaim liberty to the captives And recovery of sight to the blind, To set at liberty those who are oppressed; To proclaim the acceptable year of the Lord." Luke 4:17-19 (Italics added)

Christ Is Our Pastor
"Shepherd the flock of God which is among you, serving as overseers, not by compulsion but willingly, not for dishonest gain but eagerly; nor as being lords over those entrusted to you, but being examples to the flock; and when the *Chief Shepherd* [Pastor] appears, you will receive the crown of glory that does not fade away." 1 Peter 5:2-4 (Italics and Parenthesis added)

Christ Is Our Teacher
"This man came to Jesus by night and said to Him, Rabbi, we know that You are a *Teacher* come from God; for no one can do these signs that You do unless God is with him." John 3:2 (Italics added)

Every ministry (including that of the Five-Fold) is an extension of the ministry of Christ Himself, who is the Chief Cornerstone of the Foundations "...God's household, built on the foundation of the Apostles and Prophets, with Christ Jesus Himself as the Chief Cornerstone." Ephesians 2:19-20 - The foundation of the Church *is not built upon* the Apostles and Prophets themselves, but is predicated upon the revelation of Jesus Christ given by them:

"For this reason I, Paul, the prisoner of Christ Jesus for you Gentiles--if indeed you have heard of the dispensation of the grace of God which was given to me for you, *how that by revelation He made known to me the mystery* (as I have briefly written already, *by which, when you read, you may understand my knowledge in the mystery of Christ*), which in other ages was not made known to the sons of men, *as it has now been revealed by the Spirit to His holy apostles and prophets:*" Ephesians 3:1-5 (Italics added)

Ephesians 4:11-13 also indicates that these two ministries still continue in that foundational role, so it is vital for us to understand how each of these ministries work:

"And He Himself gave some to be apostles, some prophets, some evangelists, and some pastors and teachers, *for the equipping of the saints* for the work of ministry, *for the edifying of the body of Christ, till we all come* to the unity of the faith and of the knowledge of the Son of God, to a perfect man, to the measure of the stature of the fullness of Christ;" Ephesians 4:11-13 (Italics added)

God's Timetable

As we read the Word of God, we realize that there is a timetable set to all things, and without a doubt we can all testify that truly we are at the end of the age, when we are about to see the culmination of all things.   In the book of Acts, Peter speaking by the Holy Spirit on the day of Pentecost, declared this about Jesus:

"Whom heaven must receive until the times of restoration of all things, which God had spoken by the mouth of all His holy Prophets since the world began." Acts 3:21

However, in the book of Ephesians, we see something of great importance to the Body of Christ, as we seek to lay hold of end-time reality. Let me paraphrase Ephesians 4:1-14

> *Paul, by the Holy Spirit, is saying here that Jesus first descended into the lower parts of the earth; and then He rose again (or ascended) far beyond what we know to be the heavens. He is now seated on the right hand of the Father, in order that He might fulfill all things, which God had spoken, by the mouth of all His holy Prophets since the beginning of time. But the only way that Jesus can accomplish this is by manifesting Himself through His body, the Church. It is for this reason, before He ascended on high, that He did just like Elijah of old, who passed on his mantle to the young and vibrant man named Elisha. The only difference is that instead of Jesus passing His mantle on to one man, He passed it on to a many-membered man, which is His Church. In reality, Jesus tore His mantle into five different parts, namely, Apostles, Prophets, Evangelists, Pastors and Teachers. This exercise was done with only one purpose in mind, and that is for the Church to be perfected in one, thereby manifesting God's glory over all the earth.*

Why The Need For Restoration?

This word "restoration" conveys a very notable meaning in the Greek. It is the word "*apokatastasis*" (ap-ok-at-as-tas-is), which means: "the establishment of something more or better than its original."

The portion of scripture in Acts 3:21 alludes to two things before the Second Coming of Jesus.

1. That things would digress into a state of chaos and disorder from the way He left it or intended it to be.

2. He would ensure that before His return everything would be established better than its original state.

In the light of this, there is need for us to take a panoramic view of the Church, in order to arrive accurately at our destination.

The Early Church - We see the Church being launched in power in Acts 2:1-3, as the Holy Spirit descends upon the Apostles and the other saints that are gathered in the "upper room" on the eventful Day of Pentecost. From this point on, there are great signs, wonders and miracles arising out of a powerfully preached Christ.

The book of Acts records approximately the first thirty-five years of the Church's history from A.D 30 to 65. During this period, many souls were saved, including Paul, who became one of the more celebrated Apostles, because of his extensive contribution to the New Testament writings.

The next record we have is from the early Church fathers, recording events from about A.D 120. Subsequently, the period of the Church's history from around A.D 65 to 120 is missing.

The Decline of the Church - From the records of the early Church fathers; there was a drastic deviation from the Church that was recorded in the book of Acts. The period unaccounted for has been widely accepted by Theologians and Church leaders, as the "dark ages of the Church. "However, it was just before his death that Paul made this prophetic statement to the elders of the Church at Ephesus:

"And from Miletus he sent to Ephesus and called for the elders of the Church. And when they had come to him, he said to them. 'You know, from the first day that I came to Asia, in what manner I always lived among you, serving the Lord with all humility, with many tears and trials which happened to me by the plotting of the Jews; how I kept back nothing that was helpful, but proclaimed it to you, and taught you publicly and from house to house, testifying to Jews, and also to Greeks, repentance toward God and faith toward our Lord Jesus Christ. And see, now I go bound in the spirit to Jerusalem, not knowing the things that will happen to me there, except that the Holy Spirit testifies in every city, saying that chains and tribulations await me. But none of these things move me; nor do I count my life dear to myself, so that I may finish my race with joy, and the ministry which I received from the Lord Jesus, to testify to the gospel of the grace of God. And indeed, now I know that you all, among whom I have gone preaching the kingdom of God, will see my face no more. Therefore I testify to you this day that I am innocent of the blood of all men. For I have not shunned to declare to you the whole counsel of God. *Therefore take heed to yourselves and to all the flock, among which the Holy Spirit has made you overseers, to shepherd the Church of God which He purchased with His own blood. For I know this, that after my departure savage wolves will come in among you, not sparing the flock. Also from among yourselves men will rise up, speaking perverse things, to draw away the disciples after themselves.'"* Acts 20:17-30 (Italics added)

In our study of Church history we can observe the persecution and decline of the Church. During the period between A.D 120 and A.D 315 under the Roman Empire, Christianity was outlawed and banished. Also, during that time, several edicts were passed which included orders to burn all bibles and destroy all Church buildings. From that period onward, the Church, as it was known in the book of Acts, was drastically changed and succumbed to a state of apostasy. The Church then went through a millennium of darkness, slavery and deterioration.

Understanding God's Restorative Process And Order

As stated earlier, the word restoration is the Greek word *"apokatastasis"* (ap-ok-at-as-tas-is), which means: "the establishment of something more or better than its original." The last day Church will be better than the early Church.

"For thus says the Lord of hosts: Once more (it is a little while) I will shake heaven and earth, the sea and dry land; and I will shake all nations, and they shall come to the Desire of All Nations, and *I will fill this temple* [*speaking of the Church*] with glory, says the Lord of hosts. The silver is Mine, and the gold is Mine, says the Lord of hosts. *The glory of this latter temple* [*speaking of the last-day Church*] *shall be greater than the former, says the Lord of hosts.* And in this place I will give peace, says the Lord of hosts." Haggai 2:6-9 (Italics and Parenthesis added)

In God's restorative order, there is a reversal process, whereby the first becomes the last.

As we previously observed, during the dark ages, most of what was known in the early Church was either destroyed or hidden, especially the ministry gifts of Apostles, Prophets, Evangelists, Pastors and Teachers.

However, when the Holy Spirit began the restorative process in the Church, He did not start with the Apostles, but instead He began with the Pastors and Teachers and then went on to restore the Evangelists, Prophets and now the Apostles.

♦ In the 1500's it was Justification by Faith. Before then the Church had gone through the Dark Ages, which was characterized by tremendous persecution. It was at this point the Holy Spirit moved upon Martin Luther, to stand up against the ills of his day, and declare the word of God, without compromise.

♦ In the 1600's it was Water Baptism. Thank God for that truth being restored to the body, as we practice it today with great liberty.

♦ The 1700's saw Holiness and Sanctification restored. At that time tremendous revelation was revealed concerning our Sanctification and ability to live holy lives.

♦ The 1800's brought powerful teaching on The Second Coming of Jesus.

♦ With the 1880's came the restored truth on Divine Faith Healing. We thank God for this truth, as it has found its place forever in the Church of Jesus Christ in the earth. We can walk in divine health; we can believe the Lord for healing, and He has proven Himself repeatedly in this dimension, as many saints have experienced this tremendous blessing.

♦ At the turn of this century there was a tremendous truth restored to the body of Christ, namely The Holy Spirit Baptism and speaking with Other Tongues. This, I believe, was one of the most powerful moves of the

Spirit of God, as we saw major "Pentecostal" denominations and several independent groups, rising all over the earth, proclaiming a bold new Faith that changed the existing face of the Church.

♦ Then came the 1940's when we saw the restoration of Laying on of Hands and Personal Prophecy.

♦ In the 1950's it was Praise & Worship and Body Ministry, with Dancing. Also around that time we saw Deliverance and Evangelism break through in many areas of the body of Christ.

♦ In the 1960's demonology was the major point of understanding that was restored to the Church, where we saw tremendous release for peoples from all walks of life.

♦ The early 1970's brought Discipleship, Family Life and Church Growth.

♦ In mid to late 1970's it was the Faith Message along with Prosperity and Word Teachings.

♦ In the early 1980's we saw powerful revelation being released on the Kingdom of God, and our Dominion in Christ. This revealed to us, our place as kings and priests unto God, and gave us the power of declaration.

♦ Then came the restoration of Prophets to the body of Christ in the late 1980's and early 1990's. With this move, we saw the full restoration of modern day Prophets back to the body of Christ.

♦ Beginning in the late 1990's, and continuing up to this

time we are now seeing the full restoration of Apostles to the body of Christ. There is such a tremendous awareness of the government of God in the earth. It is producing in the people of God, the boldness and the wisdom to stand strong in the earth today. As the end-time Church must be fully equipped to do the work of the ministry that the Lord has ordained for us to even before the foundation of the world.

Apostolic Reference In Scripture

When the Church was being established; it was done upon the foundation laid by the Apostles and Prophets (Ephesians 2:20). Most people believe that the death of the early Apostles and Prophets meant that it was the end of Apostles and Prophets in the body of Christ. However, a thorough search of the scriptures establishes the fact, that there were more Apostles than the original twelve. For a brief look we can cite the following scriptures:

"Moreover, brethren, I declare to you that the gospel which I preached to you, which also you received and in which you stand, by which also you are saved, if you hold fast that word which I preached to you – unless you believed in vain. For I delivered to you first of all that which I also received; that Christ died for our sins according to the scriptures, And that He was buried, and that He rose again the third day according to the Scriptures, And that He was seen by Cephas, *then by the twelve [that is the original twelve Apostles].* After that He was seen by over five hundred brethren at once, of whom the greater part remain to the present, but some have fallen asleep. After that He was seen by James, *then by all the Apostles [I submit to you that this was referring to the other Apostles, apart from the original twelve].*

Then last of all He was seen by me also, as by one born out of due time." 1 Corinthians 15:1-8 (Italics and Parenthesis added)

"The Twelve" is a regular designation of the Apostles in the Gospels, and Paul uses it in 1 Corinthians 15:5. Its symbolic appropriateness is obvious, and recurs in such places as Revelation 21:14. The whole Matthias incident in Acts 1:15-26 is concerned with making up the number of the Twelve. Yet Paul's consciousness of Apostleship, is equally clear (1 Corinthians 1:1; 2 Corinthians 1:1; Galatians 1:1; Ephesians 1:1; Colossians 1:1; 1 Timothy 1:1; 2 Timothy 1:1; Titus 1:1). Further, there are instances in the New Testament where, others outside the Twelve are given the title. James the Lord's brother in Galatians 1:19; 2:9, and, though he was not a disciple (John 7:5), received a resurrection appearance personal to himself (1 Corinthians 15:7). Barnabas is called an Apostle in Acts 14:4, 14, and is introduced by Paul into an argument that denies any qualitative difference between his own Apostleship and that of the Twelve (1 Corinthians 9:1-6). The unknown Andronicus and Junias are called Apostles in Romans 16:7. Again in 1 Thessalonians 1:1; 2:6 Paul, describes Silvanus, Timothy and himself as Apostles.

Along with Paul and the other Apostles referred to in the preceding Scriptural text, there have been many other Apostles released into the body of Christ, since then. Earlier mention was made of Ephesians chapter four, from which some very salient points can be extracted:

"But to each one of us grace was given according to the measure of Christ's gift. Therefore He says: 'When He ascended on high, He led captivity captive, And gave gifts to men.' (Now this, 'He ascended' – what does it mean but that He also first descended into the lower parts of the earth? He who descended is also the One who ascended far above all the heavens, that He might fill all things.) And He Himself gave some to be *Apostles*, some Prophets, some Evangelists, and some Pastors and Teachers, for the equipping of the saints for the work of ministry, for the edifying of the body of Christ, *Till we all come to the unity of the faith and of the knowledge of the Son of God, to a perfect man, to the measure of the stature of the fullness of Christ;* that we should no longer be children, tossed to and fro and carried about with every wind of doctrine, by the trickery of men, in the cunning craftiness of deceitful plotting, But, speaking the truth in love, may grow up in all things into Him who is the head – Christ – From whom the whole body, joined and knit together by what every joint supplies, according to the effective working by which every part does its share, causes growth of the body for the edifying of itself in love." Ephesians 4:7–16. (Italics added)

Points to extract from Ephesians 4:7–16

♦ Jesus Himself gave the ministry gifts of Apostles, Prophets, Evangelists, Pastors and Teachers to men.

♦ These gifts were given to His body the Church.

♦ They were given for several reasons:

a. for equipping the saints in His body

b. to allow the saints to do the work of the ministry

c. for the edifying of the body of Christ

♦ The ministry gifts were to function in the body of Christ for a specific time period, until the following happens:

Gifts to function
function

a. we all come into the unity of the faith

b. we all come into the knowledge of the Son of God

c. we all come into a perfect man, to the measure of the stature of the fullness of Christ

d. we are no longer children, tossed to and fro and carried about with every wind of doctrine

e. we speak the truth in love and grow up in all things into Him who is the head, Christ.

Evidently, these things have not yet been fulfilled in the body of Christ; therefore the ministry gifts are still in operation, with specific emphasis conferred upon that of the Apostle. However, I would like to highlight the aspect of the Church coming into a *"perfect man."*

The word *"perfect"* is from the Greek word *teleios,* which is *"rendered complete".* This comes from the root word *telos* or *tello,* which means "to set out for a definite point or goal; the conclusion of an act or state; result; purpose." It is used 42 times in the New Testament. Compare the 42 generations in the first chapter of the book of Matthew and consider that 42 is 6 x 7; or can be understood as man brought to the perfection of Christ. A perfect man or a mature Church, this "new man" or "perfect man" is about to rise upon the face of the earth as we step into the "third day".

The Third-Day Church

"But, beloved, do not forget this one thing, that with the Lord one day is as a thousand years, and a thousand years is as one day." 2 Peter 3:8

We are about to step into the third day of the Church, and throughout the scriptures many significant things happened, on the third day. The purpose of this book is not to write about this, but as the Five-Fold ministry is restored to the Church, we are stepping into the third day and I believe we are about to see some significant events take place in the earth, through the Church. I believe that the Church will fulfill Ephesians 4 in the third day, as the Apostles are fully restored. Here are some examples of things that happened on the third day in scripture:

♦ **The Earth Was Created:**

"Then God said, 'Let the waters under the heavens be gathered together into one place, and let the dry land appear'; and it was so. And God called the dry land Earth, and the gathering together of the waters He called Seas. And God saw that it was good. Then God said, 'Let the earth bring forth grass, the herb that yields seed, and the fruit tree that yields fruit according to its kind, whose seed is in itself, on the earth'; and it was so. And the earth brought forth grass, the herb that yields seed according to its kind, and the tree that yields fruit, whose seed is in itself according to its kind. And God saw that it was good. So the evening and the morning *were the third day*." Genesis 1:9-13 (Italics added)

♦ **Abraham's Ultimate Test:**

"Now it came to pass after these things that God tested Abraham, and said to him, 'Abraham!' And he said, 'Here I am.' Then He said, 'Take now your son, your only son Isaac, whom you love, and go to the land of Moriah, and offer him there as a burnt offering on one of the mountains of which I shall tell you.' So Abraham rose early in the morning and saddled his donkey, and took two of his young men with him, and Isaac his son; and he split the wood for the burnt offering, and rose and went to the place of which God had told him. Then on *the third day* Abraham lifted his eyes and saw the place afar off. And Abraham said to his young men, stay here with the donkey; the lad and I will go yonder and worship, and we will come back to you." Genesis 22: 1-5 (Italics added)

♦ **God's Major Appearing To All Of Israel:**

"And the Lord said to Moses, 'Behold, I come to you in the thick cloud, that the people may hear when I speak with you, and believe you forever.' So Moses told the words of the people to the Lord. Then the Lord said to Moses, 'Go to the people and consecrate them today and tomorrow, and let them wash their clothes. And let them be ready for *the third day*. For on *the third day* the Lord will come down upon Mount Sinai in the sight of all the people.'" Exodus 19:9-11 (Italics added)

♦ **Saul's Death Was Announced:**

"Now it came to pass after the death of Saul, (Saul *represents a type of the religious system of today)* when David had returned from the slaughter of the Amalekites, and David had stayed two days in Ziklag, *on the third day*, behold it happened that a man came from Saul's camp with his clothes torn and dust on his head. So it was, when he came to David, that he fell to the ground and prostrated himself. And David said to him, 'Where have you come from?' So he said to him, 'I have escaped from the camp of Israel.' Then David said to him, 'How did the matter go? Please tell me,' And he answered, 'The people have fled from the battle, many of the people are fallen and dead, and Saul and Jonathan his son are dead also.'" [*News of the death of the religious systems of men will be announced! On the third day.*] 2 Samuel 1:1-4 (Italics and Parenthesis added)

♦ **The Rebuilding Of The Temple Was Finished:**

"So the elders of the Jews built, and they prospered through the prophesying of Haggai the Prophet and Zechariah the son of Iddo. And they built and finished it, according to the commandment of the God of Israel, and according to the command of Cyrus, Darius, and Artaxerxes king of Persia. Now the temple was finished on *the third day...*" Ezra 6:14-15a (Italics added)

♦ **Esther Put On Her Royal Apparel And Found The King's Favour:**

"Now it happened *on the third day* that Esther put on her royal robes and stood in the inner court of the king's palace, across from the king's house, while the king sat on his royal throne in the royal house, facing the entrance of the house. So it was, when the king saw Queen Esther standing in the court, that she found favour in his sight, and the king held out to Esther the golden sceptre that was in his hand. Then Esther went near and touched the top of the sceptre." Esther 5:1-2 (Italics added)

♦ **Jesus Was Launched Into His Ministry Of Miracles, Water Was Turned Into Wine:**

"*On the third day* there was a wedding in Cana of Galilee, and the mother of Jesus was there. Now both Jesus and His disciples were invited to the wedding. And when they ran out of wine, the mother of Jesus said to

Him,' They have no wine.' Jesus said to her, 'Woman, what does your concern have to do with Me? My hour has not yet come.' His mother said to the servants, 'Whatever He says to you, do it.' Now there were set there six water-pots of stone, according to the manner of purification of the Jews, containing twenty or thirty gallons apiece. Jesus said to them, 'Fill the water-pots with water,' and they filled them up to the brim. And He said to them, 'Draw some out now, and take it to the master of the feast,' And they took it. When the master of the feast had tasted the water that was made wine, and did not know where it came from (but the servants who had drawn the water knew), the master of the feast called the bridegroom. And said to him, 'Every man at the beginning sets out the good wine, and when the guests have well drunk, then the inferior. You have kept the good wine until now!' *This beginning of signs Jesus* did in Cana of Galilee, *and manifested His glory*; and His disciples believed in Him." John 2:1-11 (Italics added)

♦ **Jesus Predicts His Death And Third-Day Resurrection:**

"From that time Jesus began to show His disciples that He must go to Jerusalem, and suffer many things from the elders and chief priests and scribes, and be killed, and be *raised the third day*." Matthew 16:21 (Italics added)

♦ **Jesus Rose Again From The Dead:**

"...how God anointed Jesus of Nazareth with the Holy Spirit and with power, who went about doing good and healing all who were oppressed by the devil, for God was with Him. And we are witnesses of all things, which He did both in the land of the Jews and in Jerusalem, whom they killed by hanging on a tree. *Him God raised up on the third day, and showed Him openly,* not to all the people, but to witnesses chosen before by God, even to us who ate and drank with Him after He rose from the dead.'" Acts 10:38-41 (Italics added).

♦ **Jesus Declared That He Will Be Perfected:**

"On that very day some Pharisees came, saying to Him, 'Get out and depart from here, for Herod wants to kill You.' And He said to them, 'Go, tell that fox,' 'Behold, I cast out demons and perform cures today and tomorrow, and *the third day* I shall be perfected.'" Luke 13: 31-32 (Italics added)

Another book could be written on the "third day", but suffice it to say that we are going to hear a lot about the "third day" as the Apostles are fully restored to the Body of Christ; the Church.

Chapter Two
Apostolic Reference And Definition

In the Strong's Concordance the word "Apostle" is rendered "Apostolos" (ap-os-tol-oss) in the Greek, and conveys the following meaning: "A special messenger, a delegate, one commissioned for a particular task or role, one who is sent forth with a message. One who is sent to represent another in the power and authority of the one who sent him." In the final analysis, that person is similar to that of an ambassador.

When God calls one to be an Apostle, He releases His power and authority upon that individual, commissions and sends that person to function.

Apostolic Commissioning And Sending

"And when He had called His twelve *disciples* to Him,

He gave them power over unclean spirits, to cast them out, and to heal all kinds of sickness and all kinds of disease. Now the names of the twelve *Apostles* are these: first, Simon, who is called Peter, and Andrew his brother; James the son of Zebedee, and John his brother; Philip and Bartholomew; Thomas and Matthew the tax collector; James the son of Alphaeus, and Lebbaeus, whose surname was Thaddaeus; Simon the Cananite, and Judas Iscariot, who also betrayed Him. These twelve Jesus *sent out and commanded them, saying*: 'Do not go into the way of the Gentiles, and do not enter a city of the Samaritans. But go rather to the lost sheep of the house of Israel. And as you go, preach, saying, The kingdom of heaven is at hand. Heal the sick, cleanse the lepers, raise the dead, cast out demons. Freely you have received freely give. Provide neither gold nor silver nor copper in your money belts. Nor bag for your journey, nor two tunics, nor sandals, nor staffs; for a worker is worthy of his food. Now whatever city or town you enter, inquire who in it is worthy, and stay there till you go out. And when you go into a household, greet it. If the household is worthy, let your peace come upon it. But if it is not worthy, let your peace return to you. And whoever will not receive you nor hear your words, when you depart from that house or city, shake off the dust from your feet. Assuredly, I say to you, it will be more tolerable for the land of Sodom and Gomorrah in the day of judgement than for that city!'" Matthew 10:1-15 (Italics added).

Principles Set By Jesus

From Disciple To Apostle - Matthew 10:1-2

Verse 1 declares that Jesus calls His twelve disciples – Greek word "mathetes" which means, pupil or learner – and in verse 2 they are called Apostles - "Apostolos" (ap-os-tol-oss) in the Greek, and conveys the following meaning: "A special messenger, delegate, one commissioned for a particular task or role, one who is sent forth with a message. One who is sent to represent another in the power and authority of the one who sent him/her."

So essentially, the disciples became Apostles as they were sent and commissioned, and given a release of power by Jesus. This is the first place we see the Apostles emerging, and we can extract some principles from this first release.

| Apostolic Principles: Matthew 10: 5-42 |

1. In verses 5-6 the Apostles are given "*very clear directions*" From this we can glean that the Apostolic call must be accompanied with a specific mandate and vision.

2. In verse 7 they are instructed to preach "*the kingdom.*" There must be a relevant kingdom message preached by the Apostles in this time.

3. In verse 8 "*miracles, signs and wonders*" are to be accomplished by the Apostles. This is one of the pillars of the Apostolic, which will be dealt with later.

4. Whenever God gives vision, *provision is made.* In verses 9-10 promise of provision is made.

5. The Apostolic is committed to that *which is worthy.* In verse 11-13 careful inquiries are to be made for that which is worthy.

6. In verses 14-15 the Lord promises that any *refusal of the Apostles' kingdom message* will end in disaster.

7. The Lord releases *divine wisdom* as He sends out the Apostles, verse 16. Wisdom is another pillar of the Apostolic, and will be dealt with later.

8. In verses 17-18; 21-23 the Lord warns them about *persecutions*, declaring that it cannot be avoided.

9. Apostles are given *divine revelation*, as promised in verse 19-20; 26-27.

10. Verses 24-25 *identify the Apostles with their source*, from the perspective that they should be encouraged, and not lose heart because of any adverse situation.

11. Luke 11: 28 makes this statement - "for which of you, intending to build a tower, does not sit down first and count the cost, whether he has enough to finish it." We see this same dynamics of *Apostolic cost*, in verses 34-39.

12. Verses 40-42 speak about *Apostolic reward*, declaring that there are tremendous blessings and rewards in receiving the Apostles.

Before proceeding, I would like to take a look at some of the things Apostles and the Apostolic Movement is not:

♦ Apostles are not superhuman.

♦ Apostles are not dictatorial rulers.

♦ Apostles are not Christian Popes.

♦ The Apostolic movement that is emerging is not some super structure that will dominate and rule the body of

Christ.

The First Principle

One of the areas of major concern, as the Lord restores Apostles to His body, is referred to as "The First Principle".

This is taken from primarily two texts of scripture:

"And God has appointed these in the Church; *first Apostles*, second Prophets, third Teachers, after that miracles, then gifts of Healings, helps, administrations, various kinds of tongues." 1 Corinthians 12:28 (Italics added)

"And He Himself gave some to be *Apostles*, some Prophets, some Evangelists, and some Pastors and Teachers." Ephesians 4:11 (Italics added).

In 1 Corinthians 12:28 the word used for "*first*" is the Greek word "*proton*" and it is rendered: "first in time, place, order or importance." It is also rendered: "before, at the beginning, or chiefly." In Ephesians 4:11 "*Apostles*" are mentioned first in the listing of the five ministry gifts; and because of this, some have declared that it carries the same connotation as in 1 Corinthians 12:28.

In light of this, the view is emerging in some quarters that the Apostle is the greatest ministry, and should have pre-eminence over all other ministers and ministries. Also, some have perceived this in the context of earthly patterns of leadership, and are patterning themselves after the order of earthly Rulership. Accordingly, they have begun to act and function similar to some CEO's and Managing Directors of major earthly organizations and are seeking to "Lord it over

God's people." They apply earthly management principles that sound and look good", but divert the saints from dependence on the Holy Spirit to dependence on the arm of flesh.

The Holy Spirit's Intent

It was never the Holy Spirit's intent to bring a separation among the ministry gifts given by Christ, in 1 Corinthians 12:28 and Ephesians 4:11. Doing so would have been impossible, because it would have separated the godhead of Father, Son and Holy Spirit according to rank. As was said earlier, the ministry gifts of Apostles, Prophets, Evangelists, Pastors and Teachers are all extensions of the Christ anointing - in essence they are one and the same with Christ. This is similar to the godhead, they are one, and do not compete against each other because of perceived ranking.

Leadership in the body of Christ was never purposed to "*lord it*" over people, but rather for supporting and under-girding. Peter, writing to the elders and leaders of the Church exhorted them, saying:

> "To the elders who are among you I exhort, I who am a fellow elder and a witness of the sufferings of Christ, and also a partaker of the glory that will be revealed: Shepherd the flock of God which is among you, serving as overseers, not by compulsion but willingly, not for dishonest gain but eagerly; nor as being lords over those entrusted to you, but being examples to the flock; and when the Chief Shepherd appears, you will receive the crown of glory that does not fade away." 1 Peter 5:1–4

Peter makes at least three salient points as follows:

♦ Function as an elder not by compulsion but willingly.

♦ Do not build a financial empire for oneself through dishonest gain or greed.

♦ Do not dominate or lord it over the people, but serve as examples.

Domination:

Dominion has always been a trap for many leaders in the moves of God, and in the Apostolic, it is again one of the traps. Normally, as the move of God is initiated, certain men are positioned at the forefront of the move, but some of these forerunners tend to claim ownership of the move. The latter category of individuals treats the move of God as its personal business, and applies principles of the world to bring success. Jesus dealt with this issue when He walked the face of the earth, and it will do well for us to keep referring to what He had to say about it. A classic case was that of the mother of Zebedee's sons:

"Then the mother of Zebedee's sons came to Him with her sons, kneeling down and asking something from Him. And He said unto her, 'What do you wish?' She said to Him, 'Grant that these two sons of mine may sit, one on Your right hand and the other on the left, in Your kingdom.' But Jesus answered and said, 'You do not know what you ask. Are you able to drink the cup that I am about to drink, and be baptized with the baptism that I am baptized with?' They said to Him, 'We are able.' So He said to them, 'You will drink indeed My cup, and be baptized with the baptism that I am baptized with; but to sit on My right hand, and on My left is not Mine to give, but it is for those for whom it is prepared by My Father.' And when the ten heard it, they were greatly displeased with the two brothers. But Jesus called them to Himself and said, 'You know that the rulers of the Gentiles lord it over them, and those that are great exercise authority over them. Yet it shall not be so among you; but whoever desires to become great among you, let him be your servant. And whoever desires to be *first* [*this is the same Greek word "proton"*] among you, let him be your slave - just as the Son of man did not come to be served, but to serve, and to give his life a ransom for many.'" Matthew 20:20–28 (Italics and Parenthesis added)

Jesus was clearly laying down the pattern for leadership in the Church, and it was not to be in the same vein as that of the world. In fact, anytime this kind of dictatorial rule surfaces in the Church, it grieves the Holy Spirit. The issue of "authority" is one of the pillars of the Apostolic which will be discussed later; however, please note that a sure sign of "false Apostles" is a tendency for dictatorial rule, as described by the Apostle Paul:

"For I consider that I am not at all inferior to the most eminent Apostles. Even though I am untrained in speech, yet I am not in knowledge. But we have been thoroughly manifested among you in all things. Did I commit sin in humbling myself that you might be exalted, because I preached the gospel of God to you free of charge? I robbed other Churches, taking from them wages to minister to you. And when I was present with you, and in need, I was a burden to no one, for what I lacked the brethren who came from Macedonia supplied. And in everything I kept myself from being burdensome to you, and so I will keep myself. As the truth of Christ is in me, no one shall stop me from this boasting in the regions of Achaia. Why? Because I do not love you? God knows! But what I do, I will also continue to do, that I may cut off the opportunity from those who desire an opportunity to be regarded just as we are in the things of which we

boast. *For such men are false Apostles, deceitful workers, transforming themselves into Apostles of Christ.* And no wonder! For satan himself transforms himself as an angel of light. Therefore it is no great thing if his ministers also transform themselves into ministers of righteousness, whose end will be according to their works. I say again, let no one think me a fool. If otherwise, at least receive me as a fool, that I also may boast a little. What I speak, I speak not according to the Lord, but as it were, foolishly, in this confident boasting. Seeing that many boast according to the flesh, I also will boast. *For you put up with fools gladly, since you yourselves are wise! For you put up with it if one brings you into bondage, if one devours you, if one takes from you, if one exalts himself, if one strikes you on the face.* To our shame I say that we were too weak for that! But in whatever anyone is bold – I speak foolishly – I am bold also." 2 Corinthians 11:5–21 (Italics added).

Paul was making a stand for his Apostolic call and function, as he was being accused of being a weak leader.   The Corinthian Church was being taught that Paul's inability to orate with great eloquence and his gentleness among them, among other things, were signs of his weakness as a leader. He responds by pointing out to them, that the only reason he was being accused as weak, was that he did not lord it over them and put them in bondage, thereby taking advantage of them. In fact, he ascribed that kind of behaviour and mentality to that of false Apostles. And we can most certainly do the same.

Another point to note – These two scriptural texts do not concur with the prevailing view held by some, that the listing of Apostles first, automatically suggests that the Apostle is the greatest ministry gift and should be given pre-eminence. If we were to take a closer look at the structure of these two texts, we will see that while Ephesians lists the Teachers fifth, Corinthians lists them third. Please note that these two scriptural texts are the only ones listing the ministry gifts, and they do not concur, that naming Apostles first in the lists means they are superior to any of the other ministry gifts. Therefore, it will be unwise to make that assumption.

We need to also take into account the following scriptural reference regarding Apostles.

"For I think that God hath *set forth us, the Apostles*, last, as it were appointed to death; for we are made a spectacle unto the world, and to angels, and to men". KJV 1 Corinthians 4:9 (Italics added)

Apostles are named first because God has gifted them with an anointing that could penetrate, and begin spiritual construction in any territory. "First", in this particular instance, do not mean better; but rather, it signifies the position of function. Apostles flow in foundational gifts; they have a governmental, building anointing (an anointing to establish things). Similarly, in our physical bodies the head is not better than the rest of the body because it is at the top of the body. It is a part of the whole body and therefore is united as one with every other member of the body.

1 Corinthians 12 gives an operational platform for all spiritual gifting in the body of Christ, and could be applied in the context of the Five-Fold ministry gifting of Apostles, Prophets, Evangelists, Pastors and Teachers. Another vital example as mentioned before is that of the godhead; God the Father, God the Son and God the Holy Spirit are all one. Their functions are different, but they are still one. So quintessentially, Jesus the Apostle, Jesus the Prophet, Jesus the Evangelist, Jesus the Pastor and Jesus the Teacher are all one.

satan's intent is to plant seeds of separation and disunity in the foundational stage of the restoration of Apostles to the body of Christ. He is well aware that the full restoration of Apostles will result in the unity of the body of Christ. Ephesians 4:13 declares, that one of the end results of the Five-Fold ministry gifts of Apostles, Prophets, Evangelists, Pastors and Teachers functioning together, is the *"unity of the faith"*. If the devil can cause a division because of "perceived ranking" in the Five-Fold ministry gifts, he assumes that he will stop the forward march of the Church towards unity. But as with every other move of God, the Holy Spirit will have His way, and the Apostles will be fully restored in spite of the excesses, misinterpretations and schisms intended by the devil.

Glory to God, Hallelujah we have truly entered into one of the greatest epochs in the history of the Church, for with the restoration of the Apostles, we are beginning to see a fully functional, awesome, powerful, wisdom filled, Holy Spirit filled Church standing in the earth. We will see the nations bowing to the Lordship of Jesus in His Church, and the saints doing the work of the ministry, creating the atmosphere for the return of its King and Lord, Jesus Christ. This is the first time since the book of Acts, that all five ministry gifts are operational and accepted in the body of Christ. What an awesome time to be alive, this is the generation with the greatest potential to actually defeat death, and bring Jesus back to earth. *Hallelujah!*

This end-time Church will be more powerful than the early Church in the book of Acts, because, when God restores something, He always makes it better than it was before. There is tremendous excitement in the heavens, as the Body of Christ is finally beginning to see and understand God's ultimate plan. Paul's prayer is being fully answered:

"Therefore I also, after I heard of your faith in the Lord

Jesus and your love for all the saints, do not cease to give thanks for you, making mention of you in my prayers: *that the God of our Lord Jesus Christ, the Father of glory, may give unto you the spirit of wisdom and revelation in the knowledge of Him, the eyes of your understanding being enlightened; that you may know what is the hope of His calling, what are the riches of the glory of His inheritance in the saints, and what is the exceeding greatness of His power toward us who believe, according to the working of His mighty power which He worked in Christ,* when He raised Him from the dead and seated Him at His right hand in the heavenly places, far above all principality, and power, and might and dominion, and every name that is named, not only in this age, but also in that which is to come. And He put all things under His feet, and gave Him to be head over all things to the church, which is His body, the fullness of Him who fills all in all." Ephesians 1:15–23 (Italics added).

The Man-Child Anointing

In Revelation 12 we see the woman (a type of the Church) giving birth to a man-child. I believe this to be very significant with respect to what the Holy Spirit is doing in these last days. The Church has always been referred to as a woman, or as the "bride of Christ". While this is true, during these end-times the Church must adopt a militant, warring nature (against the kingdom of darkness) to effectively bring Jesus back.

This man-child represents the nature of the anointing that has already begun to emerge in the Church. This anointing is a breakthrough, conquering, and militant type of anointing. We see in Revelation 12:5 that this man-child was to rule the nations with a rod of iron.

"She bore a male Child who was *to rule all nations with a rod of iron.* And her Child was caught up to God and His throne." Revelation 12:5 (Italics added)

This text of scripture about ruling the nations with a rod of iron is also echoed in Psalms chapter two:

"Why do the nations rage, and the people plot a vain thing? The kings of the earth set themselves, and the rulers take counsel together, against the Lord and against His Anointed, saying, 'let us break their bonds in pieces and cast away Their cords from us.' He who sits in the heavens shall laugh; the Lord shall hold them in derision. Then He shall speak to them in His wrath, and distress them in His deep displeasure: 'Yet I have set My King on My holy hill of Zion.' I will declare the decree: The Lord has said to Me, 'You are My Son, today I have begotten You. Ask of Me, and I will give You the nations for Your inheritance, and the ends of the earth for Your possession. *You shall break them with a rod of iron; You shall dash them to pieces like a potter's vessel.'* Now therefore, be wise, O kings; be instructed, you judges of the earth. Serve the Lord with fear, and rejoice with trembling. Kiss the Son, lest He be angry, and you perish in the way, when His wrath is kindled but a little. Blessed are all those who put their trust in Him." (Italics added)

What a tremendous Prophetic declaration! The nations of the earth are destined to bow to the Lordship of Jesus and His Church.

As the Apostles are fully restored to the Body of Christ, the full equipping of the saints will then be realized and the Church will enter into one of its most glorious days upon the planet. The systems of the earth are already beginning to convulse, in the political, economic, social and every other sector. A new day is about to dawn, when the saints of the Most High will possess the Kingdom.

As we proceed let us look at *five main Pillars* of the Apostolic, and explore some of the main characteristics of the Apostolic ministry and anointing.

Chapter Three
Pillar One
Spirit of Wisdom

In 1 Corinthians 3:10 we see the Apostle Paul declaring that one of the operational technologies upon Apostles is the *Spirit of Wisdom*.

"According to the grace of God which was given to me, as a *Wise-Master* builder I have laid the foundation, and another builds on it. But let each one take heed how he builds on it." (Italics added).

This dynamic of Wisdom must have its genesis in the Lord!

"There shall come forth a Rod from the stem of Jesse, and a Branch shall grow out of his roots [*Speaking of Jesus*]. The Spirit of the Lord shall rest upon Him, the *Spirit of wisdom* and understanding, the Spirit of counsel and might, the Spirit of knowledge and of the fear of the

Lord." Isaiah 11:1-2 (Italics and Parenthesis added).

"And the Child [*Jesus*] grew and became strong in spirit, *filled with wisdom*; and the grace of God was upon Him." Luke 2:40 (Italics and Parenthesis added)

It must not be rooted in the intelligence of the earth. This is very critical in the early stages of Apostolic restoration, because we will see a lot of the "wisdom" and "intelligence" of the world being introduced as "wisdom" from God, in an attempt to build inaccurately upon the foundation. Most times, wisdom from God seems, as foolishness to the world, and it must remain that way. We are not to try and simplify or clarify the moves of God, so that the world will understand. As Jesus walked with His disciples and ministered to the multitudes, He spoke in parables and afterwards He explained them to His disciples but would leave the world guessing.

"And the disciples came and said to Him, 'Why do You speak to them [*the world*] in parables?' *He answered and said to them, 'Because it has been given to you to know the mysteries of the kingdom of heaven, but to them it has not been given.* For whoever has, to him more will be given, and he will have abundance; but whoever does not have, even what he has will be taken away from him. Therefore I speak to them in parables, because seeing they do not see, and hearing they do not hear, nor do they understand.'" Matthew 13:10-13 (Italics and Parenthesis added).

There are several examples in scripture that clearly show we are not to rely on earthly wisdom for spiritual function. In the book of Proverbs, there are several passages that exalt the wisdom of God, and warn us to be careful of the wisdom of the world. Proverbs chapter nine is a classic example of the wisdom of God contrasted with the wisdom of the world, they both seem to call from the same place (the high places of the city), but their ends are very different:

"Wisdom has built her house, She has hewn out her seven pillars; She has slaughtered her meat, She has mixed her wine, She has also furnished her table. She has sent out her maidens, *She cries out from the highest places of the city,* 'Whoever is simple, let him turn in here!' As for him who lacks understanding, she says to him, 'Come, eat of my bread and drink of the wine I have mixed, Forsake foolishness and live, and go in the way of understanding.'" Proverbs 9:1-6 (Italics added).

"*The fear of the Lord is the beginning of wisdom* and the knowledge of the Holy One is understanding, For by me your days will be multiplied, and years of your life will be added to you. If you are wise, you are wise for yourself, and if you scoff, you will bear it alone. A foolish woman is clamorous; she is simple, and knows nothing. For she sits at the door of her house, *on a seat by the highest places of the city.* To call to those who pass by, who go straight on their way; 'Whoever is simple, let him turn in here;' and as for him who lacks understanding, she says to him, 'Stolen water is sweet, and bread eaten in secret is pleasant.' But he does not know that the dead are there, that her guests are in the depths of hell." Proverbs 9:10-18 (Italics added)

With the restoration of the Apostles, God will release the Church into a greater dimension of His wisdom!

Proverbs chapter eight describes the powerful nature of *wisdom*, it also describes how the Almighty God used her when He created the universe, and explains how things still exist from the foundation of the earth.

Jesus declared that God would send Prophets and Apostles (wise men). (Luke 11:49 & Matthew 23:34)

"Therefore the *wisdom of God* also said, I will send them Prophets and Apostles, and some of them they will kill and persecute." Luke 11:49 (Italics added)

"Therefore, indeed, I send you Prophets, *wise men*, [*Apostles*] and scribes; some of them you will kill and crucify, and some of them you will scourge in your synagogues and persecute from city to city." Matthew 23:34 (Italics and Parenthesis added)

As mentioned earlier, the Apostle Paul, in writing to the Corinthian Church, declared that Apostles are *wise-master builders*. Basically what he is saying is, that *wisdom* is part of the technology and equipment given to Apostles to effect God's work. Let us look at some examples of *wise-master builders*.

The Zerubbabel Example

As the Holy Spirit continues to set the parameters of operation and functionality in what needs to be accomplished for the Lord within and through the Apostles, let us take a close look at some patterns:

"Now the angel who talked with me came back and wakened me, as a man who is wakened out of his sleep… So he answered and said to me: 'This is the Word of the Lord to Zerubbabel; not by *might nor by power*, but by My Spirit, says *the Lord of hosts.* Who are you O great mountain? Before Zerubbabel you shall become a plain! *And he shall bring forth the capstone with shouts of*

Grace, Grace to it!'" Zechariah 4:1, 10 (Italics added)

Not By Might Nor By Power!

♦ The strength of man or any of his agencies will not accomplish this work. This word *might* is a very interesting Hebrew word, it is the word "chayil" and it is used in two contexts in the original:

1. To describe an army or military might - (strength, power, force, etc). Deuteronomy 11:4; Psalms 20:7

2. It is also used to describe accumulated wealth. Deuteronomy 8:17

The Lord Of Hosts!

♦ This is an awesome statement in the light of what was said before: The Lord is declaring that the work will not be accomplished by "chayil", but instead the Lord of Hosts will accomplish it. The Hebrew word for "hosts" is the word "tsaba" and it is rendered a mass of persons organized for war; an army! The Greek word for "hosts" is the word "sabaoth" and is rendered, army, a military epithet of God. In the book of Joshua we have a tremendous example of this.

Joshua was a man that was full of the *spirit of wisdom* for Apostolic leadership.

"Now Joshua the son of Nun was *full of the spirit of wisdom*, for Moses had laid his hands on him; so the children of Israel heeded him, and did as the Lord had commanded Moses." Deuteronomy 34:9 (Italics added)

It was this same *spirit of wisdom* that allowed him to effectively lead the children of Israel into the land of promise:

> *"And it came to pass, when Joshua was by Jericho, that he lifted his eyes and looked, and behold, a Man stood opposite him with His sword drawn in His hand. And Joshua went to Him and said to Him, 'Are You for us or for our adversaries?'* So He said, *'No, but as Commander [Captain] of the army of the Lord [Lord of Hosts] I have now come.' And Joshua fell on his face to the earth and worshipped, and said to Him, 'What does my Lord say to His servant?'"* Joshua 5:13-14 (Italics and Parenthesis added)

What a powerful encounter, what a tremendous revelation! The background to this encounter is that the children of Israel had been in the wilderness forty years, and had seen the hand of God in all dimensions, culminating in the death of Moses. Joshua was commissioned to lead the people forward into their inheritance; they crossed the Jordan River with its bank overflowing, and were at the very threshold of their promise.

The manna (described as *"what is it"* – no clear sense of direction and understanding) that they ate in the wilderness is now dried up, and they need a fresh sense of direction from the Lord.

Before them is an impregnable fortress in the form of Jericho, and it is at this place, Joshua comes into one of the most powerful revelations on warfare and of the taking of territory listed in the Old Testament. In order for Jericho, which was standing directly in the way to their Promised Land, to be conquered, they could not rely on *"Chayil"* (man's strength or ability) they had to rely on *"Tsaba"* or *"Sabaoth"* (the Lord of Hosts). As it was with Zerubbabel (Zechariah: 4:7) so it was with Joshua, (Jericho stood before him). Both he and Zerubbabel understood that it was not by might nor by power, but by the Spirit of the Lord of Hosts. Hallelujah!

The Capstone Or Headstone

This refers to foundational (*Apostolic*) structures. The capstone, headstone or chief cornerstone is what the entire building gets its shape and size from. This is a very critical stage in any building project; hence the reason there must be divine strength and wisdom.

Throughout the scriptures, every time the Lord was about to initiate and establish His work, the *spirit of wisdom* was sent first. In Moses' time there were men like Bezalel:

"Then the Lord spoke to Moses, saying, 'See, I have called by name Bezalel the son of Uri, the son of Hur, of the tribe of Judah. And I have *filled him with the Spirit of God, in wisdom*, in understanding, in knowledge, and in all manner of workmanship, To design artistic works, to work in gold, in silver, in bronze, in cutting jewels for setting, in carving wood, and to work in all manner of workmanship. And I, indeed I, have appointed with him Aholiab the son of Ahisamach, of the tribe of Dan; and I have put *wisdom* in the hearts of all the gifted artisans, that they may make all that I have commanded you.'"
Exodus 31:1-6 (Italics added)

Grace! Grace!

♦ This is absolutely needed, especially in the foundational stage of any work for and with the Lord. *Grace* comes from the Hebrew word *"chen"* and it also conveys *'favour'*. It is used of the action of a superior, whether human or divine, to an inferior. In this particular scriptural reference (Zechariah 4:1, 10), Zerubbabel was about to lay the foundation stone and there was tremendous opposition, and Grace was needed (this was also the case with Nehemiah, Ezra, and the early Church). In the early Church we see a dimension called Great Grace, released to the saints (Acts 4:33). In this hour of Apostolic restoration, *Great Grace* is being released to the Church.

The Moses Example

Moses presents a very interesting case as a type of the Apostolic. He was born at a time when Egypt (a type of the systems of the world), was at the height of her strength and dominance, and the people of God - Israel, were facing extinction. A decree had gone out for all the male children that were born to the Israelites, to be killed. He was saved by divine wisdom that was given to his mother by God, and was brought up in the home of the king of Egypt. He was fully trained in all the "wisdom" and culture of Egypt, but when he came of age, he understood his true identity, and submitted to the call of God to *be sent (Apostolic call)* to deliver God's people. As the Lord began to set the parameters for his function in Egypt, he declared to God that he couldn't speak. He also said that he was not eloquent (in actual fact, he was not as eloquent as his "peers" from the system in Egypt) (Exodus 4:10).

God then declares to him:

> "So the Lord said unto him, 'Who has made man's mouth? Or who makes the mute, the deaf, the seeing, or the blind? Have not I the Lord? Now therefore, go, and I will be with your mouth and teach you what you will say.'" Exodus 4:11-12

On that basis, Moses then goes into Egypt, and is used mightily of the Lord to bring deliverance to His people. He initiates the process, and throws down his rod and it turns into a snake, and then the Egyptians follow. For too long, we the Church have followed the system of the earth in constructing for the Lord. We use their management schemes and techniques; we use their inventions. The time has come for that to change. As we read through the account in the book of Exodus, we see time and time again, that the wisdom that was used to force Pharaoh's hand to free God's people, was very unconventional. It had no root in the system of Egypt.

The Daniel Example

Daniel is a tremendous Apostolic figure in the scriptures. King Nebuchadnezzar of Babylon, besieged Jerusalem, destroyed it, and took the best and the brightest to influence and strengthen his domain. His kingdom was very expansive; it covered most of the then Middle East. Daniel was taken along with his three friends and incarcerated in Babylon. *He is between the ages of 13 - 16 years and the 12 chapters of the book of Daniel span over a 65-year period.* He stood strong, as an influential figure, under four successive kings and two successive kingdoms, Babylon and Medo-Persia and remained relevant in every change.

Please understand that Daniel was initially trained in Israel. In fact, his formative years had already passed, and Babylon (a type of the religious, political, social, economic system of the world) wanted to have these boys for their use.

Even though Daniel was *trained in the language and literature of Babylon* (Daniel 1:4), it was God who gave him the wisdom to function in Babylon successfully:

"As for these four young men, *God gave* them knowledge and skill in all literature and *wisdom*; and Daniel had understanding in all visions and dreams." Daniel 1:17 (Italics added)

"There is a man in your kingdom in whom is the *Spirit of the Holy God*. And in the days of your father, light and understanding and *wisdom*, like the wisdom of the gods, were found in him; and king Nebuchadnezzar your father -your father the king- made him chief of the magicians, astrologers, Chaldeans, and soothsayers. Inasmuch as an excellent spirit, knowledge, understanding, interpreting dreams, solving riddles, and explaining enigmas were found in this Daniel whom the king named Belteshazzar, now let Daniel be called and he will give the interpretation." Daniel 5:11-12 (Italics added).

Daniel did not rely upon the "wisdom" of the Babylonians to function; he totally relied upon God's wisdom. In fact, it is very interesting to note the issue, surrounding Daniel's initial promotion. King Nebuchadnezzar had a dream that he could not remember, let alone have interpreted.

"Now in the second year of Nebuchadnezzar's reign, Nebuchadnezzar had dreams, and his spirit was so troubled that his sleep left him. Then the king gave the command to call the magicians, the astrologers, the sorcerers, and the Chaldeans to tell the king his dreams. So they came and stood before the king. And the king said to them, 'I have had a dream, and my spirit is anxious to know the dream.' Then the Chaldeans spoke to the king in Aramaic, 'O king, live forever! Tell your servants the dream, and we will give the interpretation.' The king answered and said to the Chaldeans, 'My

decision is firm: If you do not make known the dream to me, and its interpretation, you shall be cut in pieces, and your houses shall be made an ash heap. 'However, if you tell the dream and its interpretation, you shall receive from me gifts, rewards, and great honour. Therefore tell me the dream and its interpretation.' They answered again and said, 'Let the king tell his servants the dream and we will give its interpretation.' The king answered and said, ' know for certain that you would gain time, because you see that my decision is firm: 'If you do not make known the dream to me, there is only one decree for you! For you have agreed to speak lying and corrupt words before me till the time has changed. Therefore tell me the dream, and I shall know that you can give me its interpretation.' The Chaldeans answered the king, and said: 'There is not a man on earth who can tell the king's matter; therefore no king, lord, or ruler has ever asked such things of any magician, astrologer, or Chaldean.'"
Daniel 2:1-10

Of course the Lord had set the whole thing up, and there was no one in the demonic realm that could interpret the king's dream. demonic powers and principalities do not have a clue as to what the Lord is doing. They do not posses the wisdom that God has, and it is always sad when the people of God rely on "earthly wisdom" to accomplish spiritual things.

As the decree goes out, and all the wise men are sought and being killed:

"So the decree went out, and they began killing the wise men; and they sought for Daniel and his companions, to kill them." Daniel 2:13

Daniel steps up and declares Godly wisdom, far beyond

anything Babylon had ever seen:

> "Then with counsel and *wisdom* Daniel answered Arioch,
> the captain of the king's guard, who had gone out to kill
> the wise men of Babylon; He answered and said to
> Arioch the king's captain, 'Why is the decree from the
> king so urgent?' Then Arioch made the decision known
> to Daniel. So Daniel went in and asked the king to give
> him time, that he might tell the king the interpretation.
> Then Daniel went to his house, and made the decision
> known to Hananiah, Mishael, and Azariah, his
> companions, That they might seek mercies from the God
> of heaven concerning this secret, so that Daniel and his
> companions might not perish with the rest of the wise
> men of Babylon. Then the secret was revealed to Daniel
> in a night vision. So Daniel blessed the God of heaven.
> Daniel answered and said: 'Blessed be the name of God
> forever and ever, For *wisdom* and might are His. And He
> changes the times and the seasons; He removes kings and
> raises up kings; He gives *wisdom* to the wise and
> knowledge to those who have understanding. He reveals
> deep and secret things; He knows what is in the darkness,
> And light dwells with Him. I thank You and praise You,
> O God of my fathers; You have given me *wisdom* and
> might, and have now made known to me what we asked
> of You, for You have made known to us the king's
> demand.'" Daniel 2:14-23 (Italics added)

Daniel then goes on to give the dream and its interpretation
to king Nebuchadnezzar (Daniel 2:24-45). It was because of
this level of *wisdom* that did not exist in all the domain of
Babylon that Daniel was promoted. No one possessed that
level. The strength of the world had no clue what to do.
demonic wisdom was useless at this level:

"Then king Nebuchadnezzar fell on his face, prostrate before Daniel, and commanded that they should present an offering and incense to him. The king answered Daniel, and said, 'Truly your God is the God of gods, the Lord of kings, and a revealer of secrets, since you could reveal this secret.' *Then the king promoted Daniel and gave him many great gifts; and he made him rule over the whole province of Babylon, and chief administrator over all the wise men of Babylon.* Also Daniel petitioned the king and he set Shadrach, Meshach, Abed-Nego over the affairs of the province of Babylon; *but Daniel sat in the gate of the king.*" Daniel 2:46-49 (Italics added)

This is the dimension of *wisdom* that is returning to the Church with the restoration of the Apostles.

Another dimension of the Spirit of wisdom is for decoding the mysteries of God, bringing illumination to the Church:

"Therefore I also, after I heard of your faith in the Lord Jesus and your love for all saints, do not cease to give thanks for you, making mention of you in my prayers: that the God of our Lord Jesus Christ, the Father of glory, may give to you *the spirit of wisdom and revelation in the knowledge of Him, the eyes of your understanding being enlightened*; that you may know what is the hope of His calling, what are the riches of the glory of His inheritance in the saints, and what is the exceeding greatness of His power toward us who believe, according to the working of His mighty power which He worked in Christ when He raised Him from the dead and seated Him at His right hand in the heavenly places, far above all principality and power and might and dominion, and every name that is named, not only in this age but also in that which is to come. And He put all things under His feet, and gave Him to be head over all things to the church, which is His body, the fullness of Him who fills all in all." Ephesians 1:15-23 (Italics added).

"For this reason I, Paul, the prisoner of Christ Jesus for you Gentiles-if indeed you have heard of the dispensation of the grace of God which was given to me for you, how that by revelation He made known to me the mystery (as I have briefly written already, by which, when you read, you may understand my knowledge in the mystery of Christ), which in other ages was not made known to the sons of men, as it has now been *revealed by the Spirit to His holy Apostles and Prophets*: that the Gentiles should be fellow heirs, of the same body, and partakers of His promise in Christ through the gospel, of which I became a minister according to the gift of the grace of God given to me by the effective working of His power. To me, who am less than the least of all the saints, this grace was given that I should preach among the Gentiles the *unsearchable* riches of Christ, *and to make all see* what is the fellowship of *the mystery*, which from the beginning of the ages has been hidden in God who created all things through Jesus Christ; *to the intent that now the manifold wisdom of God might be made known by the Church to the principalities and powers in the heavenly places,* according to the eternal purpose which He accomplished in Christ Jesus our Lord." Ephesians 3:1-11 (Italics added)

There are some tremendous words in this passage of scripture that reveals the heart of God.

Unsearchable

This is the Greek word "anexichniastos" and it is rendered "untraceable, past finding out, doesn't leave any footprints". What, Paul is actually saying, is that the mystery of God cannot be traced, because God did not leave any footprints. There remains only one way for that level of decoding to operate, and it has to be through the "Grace Gift" of Apostles, that God has given. God Himself has to reveal the mystery, otherwise it will not be known. This is why the Apostles must be restored and accepted in the body. God has graced them with the technology to decode the mysteries that are hidden in Christ.

To Make All See

The word "see" is the Greek word, "photizo" and is rendered "to brighten up, to shine, enlighten, illuminate, bring to or give light, cause to see".

Part of the grace gifting of Apostles, is to cause the saints to see and perceive the mysteries of God. The Church is built upon the foundation laid by the Apostles and Prophets. Please understand that this foundation is not the Apostles and Prophets themselves but instead it is the revelation of Christ that is released by their ministry. The Church of Jesus Christ is shaped and is being built by the revealed word that He is speaking through these ministry gifts. It is like in the beginning as the Word of God framed the world in which we live; in like manner the Word of God that is being revealed to His Holy Apostles and Prophets is shaping us the Church:

"But He answered and said, "It is written, Man shall not live by bread alone, but every word that proceeds from the mouth of God." Matthew 4:4

"Behold what manner of love the Father has bestowed on us, that we should be called children of God! Therefore the world does not know us, because it did not know Him. Beloved, now we are children of God; and it has not yet been revealed what we shall be, but we know that when He is revealed, we shall be like Him, for we shall see Him as He is. And everyone who has this hope in Him purifies himself, just as He is pure." 1 John 3:1-3

The clearer our revelation is of Christ the more we would become like Him. This is part of the grace that is given to Apostles and that is, to reveal Christ in and to us. They want to make us see – greater clarity – the glory of God in Christ!

Manifold

The word manifold is a noteworthy Greek word. It is the word *"polupoikilos"* which is made of two Greek words *"polus"* = "much" and *"poikilos"* = "varied or multicoloured". This word conveys the meaning, that the wisdom of God is much varied and has many dimensions, and shades and colours to it. God is multifaceted and He continues to demonstrate His *"manifold wisdom"* through His Church, and this will increase through the Apostles.

The Issue Of Training: verses 4-5

Remember the Babylonian system still exists in the earth. It is just as alive, just as pernicious, just as expansionist as it was in Daniel's day. Babylon is still seeking a generation that can affect the present and the future.

The word training is also a very interesting Hebrew word. It is the word - *Gadal* - to become strong! To become valuable! To be powerful! It also defines a continuous development process of growth toward greatness.

So in this context, they were to become strong, to be used in the service of Babylon. We have seen this happen, as a lot of bright young Christians have been drawn away over the decades, into the world system, and used to promote its values. They were "trained by Babylon".

We now need to have strong Churches that can rip people out of Babylon and bring them into the kingdom.

Everything in the world's system is designed to *"train or school"* us to serve it, and to loose sight of the true realm of the kingdom of God. It is designed to cause us to become ambivalent to kingdom values and principles.

Music, Culture, Economics, Politics, etc are all designed to *"Train"* us. Even Christian circles are being bombarded and assaulted by negative mindsets; lack of faith, compromise, and the list goes on, seeking to limit the advance of the kingdom in and through us.

Remember that Daniel was a real man in the real world.

♦ Understand we are not called to separate ourselves from the world.

♦ We are not to go into some remote place and become isolated or take a vow of silence.

We are not called to wear a garb that would differentiate us from the rest of society. Remember Judas had to kiss Jesus so that the Roman soldiers could identify Him (He was just like everyone else). We are called to live in this world, but not be a part of its system. We have to live right in the mess, and not be contaminated by it. We must live with the wisdom of God, and an overcoming nature, to be successful in this present world.

In the New Testament *as the foundation of the Church was being laid, wisdom was one of the qualifications for Deacons.*

"Then the twelve summoned the multitude of the disciples and said, 'It is not desirable that we should leave the word of God and serve tables. 'Therefore, brethren, seek out from among you seven men of good reputation, *full of the Holy Spirit and wisdom*, whom we may appoint over this business.'" Acts 6:2-3 (Italics added)

"And Stephen, full of faith and power, did great wonders and signs among the people. Then there arose some from what is called the Synagogue of the Freedmen (Cyrenians, Alexandrians, and those from Cilicia and Asia), disputing with Stephen. *And they were not able to resist the wisdom and the Spirit by which he spoke.*" Acts 6:8-10 (Italics added)

Today, God once again by His Spirit is raising up wise men to lead His Church forward into the climax of the ages.

Paul's Example

The Apostle Paul was trained under the great and wise Gamaliel, a religious Teacher of the Jews, before the Lord called him. However, when Paul stepped into his Apostolic call from God, he never used or relied upon his teachings under Gamaliel as a source of wisdom for Apostolic function in building the Church of Jesus Christ. Listen to his testimony!

"For we are the circumcision, who worship God in the Spirit, rejoice in Christ Jesus, and have no confidence in the flesh, though I also might have confidence in the flesh. If anyone else thinks he may have confidence in the flesh, I more so; circumcised the eighth day, of the stock of Israel, of the tribe of Benjamin, a Hebrew of the Hebrews; concerning the law, a Pharisee; concerning zeal, persecuting the church; concerning the righteous which is in the law, blameless. *But what things were gain to me, these I have counted loss for Christ. Yet indeed I also count all things loss for the excellence of the knowledge of Christ Jesus my Lord, for whom I have suffered the loss of all things, and count them rubbish, that I may gain Christ* and be found in him, not having my own righteousness which is from the law [*or any other source*], but that which is through faith in Christ, the righteous which is from God by faith; that I may know Him and the power of His resurrection, and the fellowship of His sufferings, being conformed to His death, if, by any means, I may attain to the resurrection from the dead." Philippians 3:3-11 (Italics and Parenthesis added).

That is what gave Paul the capacity to be a *"wise-master builder"* 1 Corinthians 3:10 (Italics added).

God by His Spirit, in this hour, is releasing His divine wisdom to His Church, by the restoration of the Apostles. Be encouraged to embrace the move of God, so that we can be fully equipped to do the works of the ministry we have been ordained to.

Chapter Four
Pillar Two - Fathering

As we examine this pillar, we will understand that *fathering* is much more than the ability to teach or instruct someone. It is the God given ability and grace, to impart and reproduce life in others.

Paul, in establishing this fact, wrote to the Corinthian church the following:

"For though you might have ten thousand instructors in Christ, yet you do not have many *fathers*; for in Christ Jesus I have begotten you through the gospel". 1 Corinthians 4:15 (Italics added).

Paul was making a very salient observation of fact, which I believe is still very applicable to the present day. We have many, many instructors today, but very few genuine fathers and effective mentors.

This has been one of the most neglected dimensions in the Church. Actually God knew that it would be, so He declared before, that He would set out to have this dimension fully restored in the end-times.

> "Behold I will send you *Elijah the Prophet* before the coming of the *great and dreadful day of the Lord.* And he will turn the hearts of the *fathers* to the children, and the hearts of the children to their *fathers*, lest I come and smite the earth with a curse." Malachi 4:5-6 (Italics added)

This scripture can be applied both at the level of the natural family, and in the Church. As we look around the earth today, we can see so many children being raised in a single or non-parent environment. This, in many instances, is the continuation of a vicious cycle that has left many without proper mentoring or fathering. This area has also been neglected in the Church, and we have seen the same and sometimes greater, devastating effect, as many have been raised without proper mentoring or fathering.

We are thankful; that with the restoration of the Apostles, this is one of the areas the Holy Spirit will be strengthening. In Malachi chapter four we see the heart of the fathers, first being turned to the children. This is so very important in establishing the true qualities of the fathering dimension, being released by the Holy Spirit in these end-times. It is equally important, in this process of Apostolic restoration, that there be fathers who *want* to father, and for children to turn their hearts and desire to be fathered. It is the only way that the process would be complete.

As we mentioned before, the bible in the book of Malachi declares, that in the last days God will send Elijah. He will have the anointing to turn the hearts of the fathers' back to the children and vice versa. In the light of that, we need to explore the life of Elijah and see the "Fathering" dimension that he operated from.

Elijah And Elisha

In the book of Kings we see a tremendous example of this principle. Elijah is about to come to the end of his life and the Lord gives him his final prophetic mandate, which included anointing Elisha in his place:

"So he departed from there, and *found* Elisha the son of Shaphat, who was plowing with twelve yoke of oxen before him, and he was with the twelfth. Then *Elijah passed by him and threw his mantle on him.* 1 Kings 19:19 (Italics added)

This is an awesome revelation, as Elijah (a type of the true father) finds Elisha (a type of the true son). The scripture is careful to note, that he *"found"* Elisha, which is indicative of a process of careful seeking. Elijah then threw his mantle on Elisha, signifying a willingness to release the "baton" to another chosen vessel. Everything that happened after this was because of the initiative on Elijah's part. As we read through this account there are several things that happened, which I will briefly highlight:

1. Elisha was willing to leave what he was doing to fulfill this call. (Verse 20)

2. He was willing to leave and wisely departed from his natural parents to follow Elijah, a type of his spiritual father. (Verse 20)

3. He was willing to make personal sacrifices before stepping into this new call. (Verse 21)

4. He adopts a "servant's posture" in the relationship, even though Elijah had already cast his mantle on him.

5. Elijah created within Elisha the capacity for a double portion of his anointing, by the process he took him through. Before actually walking experientially in the "*double portion*" anointing Elisha went through the following four significant stages.

a.   Stage 1 – Gilgal

"And it came to pass, when the Lord was about to take up Elijah into heaven by a whirlwind, that Elijah went with Elisha from *Gilgal*. 2 Kings 2:1 (Italics added)

To fully understand this we need to go back and explore the reason why *Gilgal* was established.

"So it was, when all the kings of the Amorites who were on the west side of the Jordan, and all the kings of the Canaanites who were by the sea, heard that the Lord had dried up the waters of the Jordan from before the children of Israel until we had crossed over, that their heart melted; and there was no spirit in them any longer because of the children of Israel. At that time the Lord said to Joshua, 'Make flint knives for yourself, and circumcise the sons of Israel again the second time.' So Joshua made flint knives for himself, and circumcised the sons of Israel at the hill of the foreskins. And this is the reason why Joshua circumcised them; All the people who came out of Egypt who were males, all the men of war, had died in the wilderness on the way, after they had come out of Egypt. For all the people who came out had been circumcised, but all the people born in the wilderness, on the way as they came out of Egypt, had not been circumcised. For the children of Israel walked forty years in the wilderness, till all the people who were men of war, who came out of Egypt, were consumed, because they did not obey the voice of the Lord – to whom the Lord swore that He would not show to their fathers that He would give us, 'a land flowing with milk and honey.' Then Joshua circumcised their sons whom He raised up in their place; for they were uncircumcised, because they had not been circumcised on the way. So it was, when they had finished circumcising all the people that they stayed in their places in the camp till they were healed. Then the Lord said to Joshua, 'This day I have rolled away the reproach of Egypt from you.' *Therefore the name of the place is called Gilgal to this day.*" Joshua 5:1-9 (Italics added)

Gilgal represents the death of unbelief; doubt; scepticism; murmuring and disobedience. Circumcision takes place at Gilgal, and renders a complete cutting away of every hindrance that will keep us from the purpose of the Lord and acts as a memorial for the next generation. It is the place of the rolling away of reproach; it is the first place towards the "double anointing". Elijah tested Elisha to see where his heart was, and also to create in him the desire for the "double anointing." Elijah was training this young man of God. It was also the place where *Agag* [king of the Amalekites, which is translated *flesh*] was killed:

"And *Saul attacked the Amalekites*, from Havilah all the way to Shur, which is east of Egypt. He also *took Agag king of the Amalekites alive*, and utterly destroyed all the people with the edge of the sword. But Saul and the people spared Agag and the best of the sheep, the oxen, the fatlings, the lambs, and all that was good, and were unwilling to utterly destroy them. But everything

despised and worthless, that they utterly destroyed." 1
Samuel 15:7-9 (Italics added)

"Then Samuel said, "*Bring Agag king of the Amalekites*
here to me." So Agag came to him cautiously. And Agag
said, "Surely the bitterness of death is past." But Samuel
said, "As your sword has made women childless, so shall
your mother be childless among women." And *Samuel
hacked Agag in pieces before the LORD in Gilgal.*" 1
Samuel 15:32-33 (Italics added)

It was also a part of Samuel's prophetic circuit when he
judged Israel. It is the place where the accurate voice of the
Lord is heard and brings regulation to your life:

"And *Samuel judged Israel* all the days of his life. *He
went from year to year on a circuit to* Bethel, *Gilgal*, and
Mizpah, and judged Israel in all those places." 1 Samuel
7:15-16 (Italics added)

It also represents the place where *"manna" (what is it?)*
ceased and they entered into food of the Promised Land – which
is abundance:

"So *the children of Israel camped in Gilgal*, and kept the
Passover on the fourteenth day of the month at twilight
on the plains of Jericho. And they ate of the produce of
the land on the day after the Passover, unleavened bread
and parched grain, on the very same day. *Then the manna
ceased on the day after they had eaten the produce of the
land*; and the children of Israel *no longer had manna, but
they ate the food of the land of Canaan that year.*"
Joshua 5:10-12 (Italics added)

But as good as Gilgal is, we will never be able to enter into all that God has for us, unless we move on.

b. Stage 2 – Bethel

"Then Elijah said to Elisha, 'Stay here, please, for the Lord has sent me on to *Bethel.*' But Elisha said, 'As the Lord lives, and as your soul lives, I will not leave you!' *So they went down to Bethel.*" 2 Kings 2:2 (Italics added)

There are two very important scriptures that convey the significance of Bethel.

"Now Jacob went out from Beersheba and went toward Haran. So he came to a certain place and stayed there all night, because the sun had set. And he took one of the stones of that place and put it at his head, and he lay down in that place to sleep. Then he dreamed, and behold, a ladder was set up on the earth, and its top reached to heaven; and here the angels of God were ascending and descending on it. And behold, the Lord stood above it and said: I am the Lord God of Abraham your father and the God of Isaac; the land on which you lie I will give to you and your descendants. Also your descendants shall be as the dust of the earth; you shall spread abroad to the west and the east, to the north and the south; and in you and in your seed all the families of the earth shall be blessed. Behold I am with you and will keep you wherever you go, and will bring you back to this land; for I will not leave you until I have done what I have spoken to you. Then Jacob awoke from his sleep and said, Surely the Lord is in this place! This is none other than the house of God, and this is the gate of heaven! Then Jacob rose early in the morning, and took the stone that he had put at his head, set it up as a pillar, and poured oil on top of it. *And he called the name of that place Bethel*; but the name of that city had been Luz previously." Genesis 28:10-19 (Italics added)

Bethel here represents a clear revelation of the house of God, both from a corporate perspective as well as an individual one. Elisha had to come to a place of realizing, that his life was the temple of God, and as such, a gateway to heaven. It was the next step towards that "double anointing". Here we see a covenant being made to honour God, with all that Jacob possessed (verse 20-22). The second reference to Bethel is very striking.

"So Jacob came to Luz (*that is Bethel*), which is in the land of Canaan, he and all the people who were with him. And he built an altar there and called the place El Bethel, because there God appeared to him when he fled from the face of his brother. Now Deborah, Rebekah's nurse, died, and she was buried below Bethel under the terebinth tree. So the name of it was called Allon Bachuth. Then God appeared to Jacob again, when he came from Padan Aram, and blessed him. And God said to him, Your name is Jacob; your name shall not be called Jacob anymore, but Israel shall be your I name. So He called his name Israel. Also God said to him; am God Almighty. Be fruitful and multiply; a nation and a company of nations shall proceed from you, and kings shall come from your body. The land, which I gave to Abraham and Isaac, I give to you; and to your descendants after you I give this land. Then God went up from him in the place where He talked with him. So Jacob set up a pillar in the place where He talked with him, a pillar of stone; and he poured a drink offering on it, and he poured oil on it. *And Jacob called the name of the place where God spoke with him, Bethel.*" Genesis 35:6-15 (Italics added)

It is in this place that God reaffirms Jacob's name change. In the light of this, it is very important to go back and read the issue surrounding Jacob's name change (Genesis 32:22-32). Before arriving at this point, one has to confront their true identity, and if it is not in accordance with the plan of God, submit to the power of transformation, even if it means wrestling with God.

Every father that is mentoring his son must know, that there is a dimension of that training the son has to go through on his own. He must face his true nature, and allow God Himself, to regulate and change him. This is the place that you receive "power with God", this place is very pivotal in what God wants done in your life. If you fail here, you will have to go back to Gilgal and start all over again.

I speak to you sons; this is the place where your own strength and ambitions (*no matter how good they may seem*) are broken. If you will submit at this stage, then you can progress to the next two stages, which will be "*crunch time*"! Hallelujah!

c. Stage 3 – Jericho

"Then Elijah said to him, Elisha, stay here, please, for the Lord has sent me on to *Jericho*. But he said, As the Lord lives, and as your soul lives, I will not leave you! *So they came to Jericho.*" 2 Kings 2:4 (Italics added)

Jericho was the seemingly impregnable fortress that stood before Joshua and the children of Israel and their land of promise. This is the place that Joshua came into one of the greatest revelations in the scriptures.

"And it came to pass, when Joshua was by Jericho, that

he lifted up his eyes and looked, and behold, a Man stood opposite him with His sword drawn in His hand. And Joshua went to Him and said to Him, Are You for us or for our adversaries? So He said, No, *but as Commander of the army of the Lord* I have now come. And Joshua fell on his face to the earth and worshipped, and said to Him, What does my Lord say to His servant? Then the Commander of the Lord's army said to Joshua, Take your sandal off your foot, for the place where you stand is holy. And Joshua did so." Joshua 5:13-15 (Italics added)

This is where Joshua realizes that God is "*Lord Sabaoth*". It is also the place that manna "what is it" ceased. It is also the place to exercise full obedience to the strategies of the Lord, and execute the written judgements on the kingdom of darkness. This is the place that you press in (Luke 19:10-11), but make sure that your training at Gilgal and Bethel is what you live by (reproach is rolled away and your character is changed and you are Spirit-led), because this is divine purpose that you are entering into. After Jericho, Elijah takes Elisha to the final frontier of testing.

d.   Stage 4 – Jordan

"Then Elijah said to him, Stay here, please, for the Lord has sent me on to the *Jordan*. But he said, As the Lord lives, and as your soul lives, I will not leave you! *So the two of them went on*." 2 Kings 2:6 (Italics added)

Before we conclude this fourth stage, let's take a look at the significant amount of discouragement that was levelled against Elisha. From the moment he leaves Gilgal, major and significant "*men of God*" known as the "*sons of the Prophets*", began to discourage him. A lot of times, when you are called to move onto the next level in God for your life, many, sometimes significant, senior, anointed "people of God" may not even see or understand the reason for your urgency, and seeming inability to hear God. However, Elisha was careful to tell them that he was well aware of what they were saying, but he also declared to them that they should shut up! (2 Kings 2:3,5,7)

Jordan is a very significant place in our journey with God. It is the place of the legitimizing of our "call" or appointment from God with authority and anointing! It is the place where you receive your mandate and mantle!

It is the place where your ministry is released with signs, miracles and wonders. It is the place where terror is instilled in the eyes of your enemies, and awe and recognition in the eyes of those who doubted your direction. Basically, it is the place where the Lord completely exonerates and vindicates you.

"Now Elijah took *his mantle*, rolled it up, and struck the water; and it was divided this way and that, so that the two of them crossed over on dry ground. And so it was, when they had crossed over, that Elijah said to Elisha, Ask! What may I do for you, before I am taken from you? Elisha said, Please let a *double portion* of your spirit be upon me. So he said, You have asked a hard thing. Nevertheless, if you see me when I am taken from you, it shall be so for you; but if not, it shall not be so. Then it happened, as they continued on and talked, that suddenly a chariot of fire appeared with the horses of fire, and separated the two of them; and Elijah went up by a whirlwind into heaven. *And Elisha saw it*, and he cried out, My father, my father, the chariot of Israel and its horsemen! So he saw him no more. And he took hold of his own clothes and tore them into two pieces. *He also took up the mantle of Elijah* that had fallen from him, and went back and stood by the bank of Jordan. *Then he took the mantle of Elijah that had fallen from him, and struck the water,* and said, Where is the Lord God of Elijah? *And when he also had struck the water, it was divided this way and that; and Elisha crossed over.* Now when the *sons of the Prophets* who were from Jericho saw him, they said, *The spirit of Elijah rests on Elisha.* And they came to meet him, and bowed to the ground before him." 2 Kings 2:8-15 (Italics added)

This is just one of the many examples in the Bible concerning fathering and mentoring.

You can study this process in some of the following examples:

♦ Moses and Joshua

♦ Jehoiada and Joash

♦ **Jesus and the Apostles**

♦ Paul and Timothy

As we step deeper into this new millennium, there is greater awareness in the body of Christ, for the need of true fathers of the faith. We are beginning to understand that, it is vital for the Apostles to be restored, thereby releasing a fatherhood dimension into the Church.

Qualities Of True Apostolic Fathers

Again, I want to re-emphasize the point made by the Apostle Paul in writing to the church at Corinth.

"For though you might have ten thousand instructors in

Christ, yet you do not have many *fathers*; for in Christ Jesus I have begotten you through the gospel." 1 Corinthians 4:15 (Italics added)

This has become so evident in our day, as many want the role of leadership within the Body of Christ, but do not possess the heart or the ability to father. As the Apostles are restored to the Church, this is going to become a strong area of focus, as true fathers will turn their heart and attention in bringing forth children, regardless of the cost. The Holy Spirit is truly releasing technology for fathering in this hour.

In 1 Corinthians 4:15 the Apostle Paul, he himself being a true father, recognized this lack in the Body of Christ in his day, and sought to address it. He declared that there were so many who were instructors and did not possess the heart of a father. The Church today is full of religious leaders, but not many fathers. There is a cry for fathers of the faith that is being echoed throughout the realm of the spirit, and the Lord has released the spirit of Elijah to answer that cry. *I remember when I lost* my first "father of the faith" in 1983, after sitting under his tutelage for three and one half years. I began a search for another father. That was the most difficult thing to find. Men were more interested in what you were able to give to their church and ministry. This left me with a constant void inside. It was not until one day the Lord revealed Himself to me in such a tremendous way, and declared to me that through the hunger and desire I had for a father; He was creating in me a father's heart. He said everything you desire in a father, that as I raise you up, I want you to give it to the "children" that I will cause to be raised up in your life. That really liberated me and stirred my heart to new levels in God.

There are many today that have been crying out for a father, and cannot find one; I say to you that in most cases, the

Lord wants to develop in you a father's heart. There is such a tremendous grace from the Spirit of God that is causing true fathers and true children to come together in this hour. The Apostles are being restored and this fathering dimension is returning to the Church.

[1]True Apostolic Fathers vs. Traditional Religious Leaders

There are major differences between one who possesses a true father's heart and one who is a traditional religious leader. Let me offer thirteen points highlighting some of these differences.

1) ♦ **A True Apostolic Father Seeks Your Interests.**

When a true father calls, he will have your interest at heart. His immediate intent will be to find out what your needs are, and not to tell you what his needs are. As we read Paul's letters to his son Timothy, we can see Paul's deep concern for his son. He encourages him and exhorts him in the "pros and cons" of the ministry.

2) ♦ **A Traditional Religious Leader Seeks What He Can Get From You.**

A call from a religious leader usually means a request that will benefit him. A religious leader would be more interested in what can be extracted from you to build up his ministry. In most cases his needs are paramount and he will use you until the very end.

3) ♦ **A True Apostolic Father Encourages Your Faith**

---
[1] Adapted from Fathering & Mentoring by Steve Schultz

And Makes You Confident.

A true father encourages you and is continually building and strengthening your faith and your self-confidence. He makes sure that he provides good examples so that your faith can come alive in Christ, and that you are confident to walk in God and are not dependent on him.

♦ **A Traditional Religious Leader Could Flatter You And Make You Proud.**

There is a difference between flattery and encouragement. Religious leaders have been known for flattery, which only leads to pride. The tendency to flatter is so that you will always stay around them and look up to them.

♦ **A True Apostolic Father Is Interested And Involved In What The Son Does.**

A true father is very concerned and involved with what is happening in your life and the call of God upon you. He will always seek to give assistance, without looking for anything in return. He is never too busy to spend quality time with you. As a matter of fact he will always seek ways to be a blessing to you, always seek to push you into the next level of success in the plan of God for your life.

♦ **A Traditional Religious Leader Is Usually Consumed With His Work.**

A religious leader is easily recognized by his continuous emphasis on his call, his ministry and what God is doing through him. Self-centeredness becomes evident. He is also usually too busy to make time for you, and his prevailing mentality is one that says, *"if you need me you know where to find me.*"

7) ♦ **When You Are In Trouble, A True Apostolic Father Stands With You.**

A true Apostolic Father will cover you during tough times or in times when errors have been made. They understand that you are "family" and that one doesn't shoot one's wounded. A true father understands that mistakes will be made, and he allows his son to make them. He will then use that as an opportunity to train and develop his son.

8) ♦ **A Traditional Religious Leader Has Been Known To Separate From You When In Trouble.**

It has been considered that the reason he disassociates himself from you is because he feels you are no longer an asset, but a liability. A true godly father never considers you a liability – he will always consider you an asset! It is a sad fact that there are many in the Body of Christ, who feel they have been used by leadership, and discarded when their usefulness ceases (sometimes due to an error or sometimes sin) and the relationship is broken. A religious leader tends to use members for the gifting they possess, and for what can be done for the ministry, rather than for the person you are.

9) ♦ **A True Apostolic Father Has A Restorational Perspective On Things.**

There is a dimension of restoration that some people need which only a true Apostolic Father can give. In this hour, because of the abuse and lack of true fathering, there are many that have become dysfunctional, and as such, are in need of restoration. Only men, who possess, a true Apostolic Father's heart can accomplish this. As true Apostles are restored, we will see a lot of healing in this dimension.

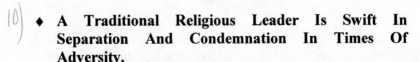

♦ **A Traditional Religious Leader Is Swift In Separation And Condemnation In Times Of Adversity.**

By contrast, dysfunctional persons have little or no chance around a religious leader. Pressure is brought upon, and the member removed, because he lacks the technology to assist these individuals. A religious leader usually does not like challenges, as he sees them as time consumers and even threatening to his self-image. Oft times it is hidden in the guise of excellence. If Jesus was primarily concerned about his image, He would not have chosen the men he did, for His Apostles.

♦ **A True Apostolic Father Disciplines.**

A true father understands the importance of discipline and is not afraid to give it. They have the destiny of their children at heart, and as such, make the necessary input to ensure that it is fulfilled. There is much reference in scripture to this effect. Here are a few:

"He who spares his rod hates his son, but he who loves him disciplines him promptly." Proverbs 13:24

"Do not withhold correction from a child, for if you beat him with a rod, he will not die." Proverbs 23:13

"The *rod and rebuke give wisdom*, but *a child left to himself brings shame* to his mother." Proverbs 29:15 (Italics added)

"Correct your son, and he will give you rest; yes, he will give delight to your soul." Proverbs 29:17

"And you have forgotten the exhortation which speaks to you as sons: '*My son, do not despise the chastening of the Lord, nor be discouraged when you are rebuked by Him; for whom the Lord loves He chastens, and scourges every son whom He receives.*' If you endure chastening, God deals with you, as with sons; for what son is there whom a father does not chasten? But if you are without chastening of which all have become partakers, then you are illegitimate and not sons. Furthermore, we have had human fathers who corrected us, and we paid them respect. Shall we not much more readily be in subjection to the Father of spirits and live? For they indeed for a few days chastened us as seemed best to them, but He for our profit, that we may be partakers of His holiness. Now no chastening seems to be joyful for the present, but painful; nevertheless, afterward it yields the peaceable fruit of righteousness to those who have been trained by it." Hebrews 12: 5-11 (Italics added)

♦ A Traditional Religious Leader Would Punish You.

A religious leader is likely to be more interested in making sure he keeps his numbers and uses methods such as punishment and "fear tactics" on his children, thereby keeping them in bondage. This usually means he does not have any long-term vision or destiny for his children apart from being in control of them.

♦ A True Apostolic Father Reproduces Himself.

A true father will reproduce himself. He will bring you to the point where you become a father. That is the whole purpose of his fathering you, so that you can rise up and father others. He is never content with just having you dependent upon him; he wants to reproduce.

◆ A Traditional Religious Leader May Create A Dependency Syndrome.

Another dimension of a religious leader is, he may create a dependency syndrome by making constant declarations such as, *"You were under me and you will always be under me! I am the one who opened doors for you to make it to where you are today!"* His aim would be to keep you emotionally and spiritually dependent upon him.   So it would not be wrong to say that he produces clones that emulate him, and not sons who imitate principles that have proven to be sound.

◆ A True Apostolic Father Ensures That You Become Better Than He Does.

I often tell my children "if they do not become better than their mother and I, then we have failed in our responsibilities as parents".   I believe that the heart of a true father longs to see his children do better than he has done.   Jesus, I believe understood this same principle when he said to His disciples:

> "Most assuredly, I say to you, he who believes in Me, the works that I do he will do also; and *greater works* than these he will do, because I go to My Father." John 14:12 (Italics added)

Since Jesus is an expression of the Father, we can see with clarity that a true father wishes his children to succeed and do *more* than he has accomplished.

◆ A Traditional Religious Leader Ensures That You

Do Not Exceed Him.

Conversely, all a religious leader is interested in, is his success, and getting his "children" to ensure that he is successful and appearing good in the sight of everyone else. A Religious leader can be compared to Saul - he becomes somewhat fearful when those "younger" (not necessarily in age) get more attention, more popularity and more anointing. As we read through the account of David's life, (Chapters 16-31 of 1 Samuel) we see that Saul was to function as a "mentor and father" to him. However, Saul became threatened and jealous because of the success of the young David, and often tried to kill him.

Sad to say, there are many leaders in the Church who demonstrate this same "Saul spirit syndrome." They are threatened, and become very insecure with the success of their children. However, as the Apostles are restored, this will change, as we will see true fathers restored to the Church.

♦ **A True Apostolic Father Understands The Concept Of Teamwork.**

A true father understands the concept of teamwork. He believes in what we will call the "football team" concept. The team has a captain and submits to his leadership. They will practice together, and play together, thereby creating a working unit. In a competition, when a touchdown is made, it is not for the benefit of the captain; it is for the entire team. The glory does not go to the person making the touchdown alone; it goes to the entire team. True fathers build on this concept, and will not seek self-glory.

♦ **A Traditional Religious Leader Loves The One-Man Syndrome.**

Quite in contrast, a religious leader's concept of team ministry, can best be described as the "golfer and his caddy concept." The golfer is the captain, and the caddy assumes the role of the team. Anyone who has ever watched or played professional golf knows that a caddy is a great asset. A good caddy knows how to play the game and knows the rules of the game. He knows which club to use, and knows how to read the greens. Even with all this knowledge and ability, the caddy never gets the opportunity to play in a competition. All he does is carry the clubs for the golfer, hand out the clubs and clean the golf balls.

Many of today's Church leaders profess that they believe in "team ministry" but if you look deep enough, you will find out that they are still in the "golfer and his caddy" syndrome. They think they head a team, but the truth of the matter is, they are the golfers and everyone else is their caddy. So just like a golfer, when the leader succeeds, his caddy is hardly ever recognized, as all the glory goes to the golfer.

♦ **There Is A Feeling Of Protection And Comfort When You Are In The Presence Of A True Apostolic Father.**

In the presence of a true father you can be free to express yourself without being afraid that you will be rebuked, for saying something he considers negative or wrong. You don't have to be looking over your shoulder and making sure that you "dot your "i"; and cross your "t."" Instead, there is that feeling of comfort, protection and freedom.

♦ **An Uneasy, Uncomfortable And Sometimes Fearful Feeling Is Experienced When In The Presence Of A Traditional Religious Leader.**

On the other hand, when in the presence of a religious leader, you may feel as though your every word and action is being scrutinized. This would feel uncomfortable, and in those moments, you will be focussed on finding a way to please the leader. There could even be times when, because of something you say or do (because of your uncertainty about how to act in his presence); he becomes very abusive and even insulting. At that time all you want to do is to reach "spiritual age" when you can leave his house. It is similar in the realm of the natural family, when a father becomes abusive and threatens his son; he leaves home as soon as it is possible. That sense of being in a family departs when this kind of treatment is meted out. I have seen followers of some leaders function and obey out of sheer fear, and make statements like "I am making sure I do what he wants because I do not want to be embarrassed in front of everyone", or "I have seen how he has treated that brother or sister, and I do not want that to happen to me, so I am making sure I do not leave room for that to happen to me." Naturally then, it would become extremely difficult to live under these kinds of conditions, and eventually *men-pleasers* would be created, instead of true, genuine sons.

♦ A True Apostolic Father Is Never Afraid To Acknowledge When He Has Made An Error.

A true father is very transparent when dealing with his son, and is not afraid to admit to mistakes or errors. He uses those times as tools to effectively train his son. He is never afraid to admit to any area of weakness. He even tries to assist the son in dealing with similar areas that maybe present in him. Paul in his writings described the struggles he had, as coming to grips with the things of God. He even went as far as to declare that he had a "thorn in his flesh."

♦ A Traditional Religious Leader Is Never Wrong.

A Religious Leader is never wrong and he will declare this fact to you. He usually does not admit to any area of weakness or error, so his followers see him as "infallible" and he makes sure that false image stays. What he is really accomplishing is giving his son a wrong impression. He could be compared to the Scribes and Pharisees but will hardly admit it. In fact he may even at times declare he is fighting against that "Pharisee spirit," when in fact he possesses it.

♦ **A True Apostolic Father Will Love And Bless You Even If You Depart From Them.**

In separation, a true father will assist you even if you are not going to be involved with his ministry anymore. He will even continue to seek to support you after your departure, and to offer whatever assistance you may need.

♦ **A Traditional Religious Leader Could Cut You Off, If You Decide To Leave Him.**

Conversely, a religious leader has also been known to develop what can be termed a "Mafia spirit." Like the Mafia, he establishes the unwritten criteria that it is all right to join him, but if you ever attempt to leave, you will be destroyed. Once you decide to leave, he will likely make attempts to character-assassinate you. He may even take things you said or did, distort it and spread those distorted (or in some cases totally fabricated) stories and falsehoods with the intention of making others reject you. It is very sad when you have to depart from a "*father's house*" under those conditions.

♦ **A True Apostolic Father Allows You To Establish New Relationships.**

A true father allows his son to establish and develop new

relationships. He is not a "control freak" and can allow other ministries to make inputs into his son's life. A true father knows and is confident in his son, because he knows the training he has imparted to his son and that he will be able to discern between truth and error. Notwithstanding this, a true father will also be available to give advice and counsel in the establishing of these new relationships.

◆ **A Traditional Religious Leader Is A "Control Freak," He Wants To Control Your Relationships.**

Some religious leaders are "control freaks" and cannot accept their "children" receiving from any other source but themselves. There are even some in "Apostolic circles" who are already developing the teaching that you can only have one Apostolic source, and this has to be handled with care. The body of Christ has always been very diverse and relationships among the different "streams or flows" are always encouraged.

The Heart Cry Of True Apostles

In this final hour, God is raising up true fathers who will have a heart for the Church, and a desire for Christ to be formed in the people of God. As we study the lives of the early Apostles, we can continue to extract tremendous principles and technologies for functioning of today's Apostles. Hear the heart cry of some of these early Apostles:

The Apostle Paul

"My little children, for whom I labour in birth again until Christ is *formed* in you." Galatians 4:19 (Italics added)

Here, the Apostle Paul is pouring out his heart to the saints in the church he had planted in Galatia. As we read through the book of Galatians, we see his true heart. Paul was literally in birth pangs, just like a pregnant woman who is about to give birth. He described his heart as to that of being in "birth pangs" so that Christ could be *"formed"* in the saints.

That word *"formed"* is the Greek word *"morphoo,"* which is rendered "to transform or completely change something from its original state." So, what Paul was saying is that he wanted to see the very nature and character of Christ, formed in the saints. He wanted them to be completely transformed, and to this end he was in constant travail and labour.

"Now for the third time I am ready to come to you. And I will not be burdensome to you; for I do not seek yours, but you. For the children ought not to lay up for the parents, but the parents for the children. And I will very gladly spend and be spent for your souls; though the more abundantly I love you, the less I am loved. But be that as it may, I did not burden you. Nevertheless, being crafty, I caught you by cunning! Did I take advantage of you by any of those whom I sent to you? I urged Titus, and sent our brother with him. Did Titus take advantage of you? Did we not walk in the same spirit? Did we not walk in the same steps? Again, do you think that we excuse ourselves to you? We speak before God in Christ. But we do all things, beloved, for your edification." 2 Corinthians 12:14-19

Here again we see the heart of a true father of the faith, absolutely concerned for the well being of his children. He is not primarily concerned with his "ministry" or even the fact that he was their "spiritual head." His concern is for their edification and building up.

In Apostle Peter's writing, you hear the heart of a true father as he encourages, instructs and admonishes those in his care. One such example is found in the following text:

> "The elders who are among you I exhort, I who am a fellow elder and a witness of the sufferings of Christ, and also a partaker of the glory that will be revealed. Shepherd the flock of God, which is among you, serving as overseers, not by compulsion but willingly, not for dishonest gain but eagerly; nor as being lords over those entrusted to you, but being examples to the flock; and when the Chief Shepherd appears, you will receive the crown of glory that does not fade away." 1 Peter 5:1-4

The Apostle John in his writings conveys the same spirit and heart of a true father of the faith. In his letters he addressed the brethren as *"my little children."* (1 John 2:1)

In his three epistles he writes to encourage, instruct and warn "his children," with the view that they keep themselves pure, and enter into all that God has for them.

As I conclude this chapter on fathering, let me say that some may say that we cannot have true fathers without true children, and that is accurate. However the Lord was very clear in the book of Malachi 4:5-6 which states:

> "Behold, I will send you Elijah the Prophet before the coming of the great and dreadful day of the Lord. And he will *turn the hearts of the fathers to the children*, and the heart of the children to *their* fathers. Lest I come and strike the earth with a curse." (Italics added)

Please note that the onus is upon the fathers to have their hearts turned first. As this happens, then the hearts of the children will be turned to *their fathers*. I declare to you that as the Apostles are restored to the Body of Christ, we are going to see many more genuine "father and son" relationships develop and nurture. This is a much-needed dimension in the Church, and I encourage you men that have been called to be fathers, to rise up and take your place in the move of God.

I would also like to establish this fact, to bring clarity and balance to the teaching on fathering and mentoring. It is possible and acceptable that there are many that are functioning, and can function, in the will and purpose of God for their lives, without a father or mentor. Several heroes in the Bible did great exploits for the Lord, and did not have a "spiritual father or mentor". To name a few, you can look at the life of Noah; Moses; Abraham and Paul. These men functioned under very strong anointings, and fulfilled the will and purpose of God for their lives, and did not have a father or mentor.

Some may argue that Moses had Jethro, but Jethro was only used to give Moses some advice, after he was already functioning in his call. Jethro was not present in the making of the man Moses, before God commissioned him to be the deliverer of the Israelites.

However, God knew that this would have been an issue in the last days, so He spoke through the Prophet Malachi, and declared that there will be a fathering spirit released into the earth at this time.

So if you are called to, or are already functioning in the office of an Apostle, this is one of the areas that will become very evident as time progresses.

Chapter Five
Pillar Three
Government and Authority

This is one of the most volatile areas of the Christian Church, and one that needs to be addressed. As we step into this realm, there are some important things that we must understand.

As this Apostolic restoration continues, some camps have already taken the principle of authority and submission, to "*bondage levels*". Some camps are only preaching church government and divine order (regardless of the title they give it), and while this is good, there needs to be some divine balance. This is needed, because some men have gone to the extreme, and are playing God with people's lives. Some saints cannot do anything unless "*their Apostle*" approves.

Many of us have been burned or abused by these kinds of ministers, but I believe that it was necessary in our development in God. God always uses both the positive and negative learning environment. We must also understand that all authority belongs to Jesus Christ. All authority, whether domestic, civil or ecclesiastical, is delegated authority. It belongs to Jesus. As He was about to step back into His true place with the Father, remember that Jesus brought Himself under the curse, to set us free from the curse. In Galatians chapter three, He made a very powerful and relevant statement. He also declared:

"And Jesus came and spoke to them, saying, '*All authority has been given to Me in heaven and on earth.*'" Matthew 28:18 (Italics added)

If a Five-Fold minister, a husband or even an extra-local minister to the churches has to bully people; his "authority" may not be genuine. *Psychic manipulation, fear tactics and intimidation have no place in the life of the believer or the Church of Jesus Christ.*

Please understand that the foundational ministries of Apostles and Prophets must be what we call "*servant-leaders*" to the Body of Christ, His Church. We must be willing as Apostles and Prophets to be submitted to the eldership of the local church. The local church is autonomous; that is, it is self-governing, free, independent and self-producing. Please also understand that there are three entities that are sovereign upon the planet:

♦ Man's volition.
♦ The home (marriage).
♦ The local church.

Foundational ministries, Apostles and Prophets, need to learn again how to be *servant-leaders* to the churches. It is always a sad thing to see how some local churches operate in relationship to "their Apostle." Some of them cannot make any decision without "their Apostle" first knowing about it. True Apostles will not make saints dependent on them; they will eventually work themselves out of a job, as they are to function "until": signifying that there will be an end to their function. Please re member that all authority centers on Jesus. True authority is never dictatorial; it is only recognized as it serves, and can only work through personal relationships.

We know that there are parallels between the Old Testament ministry and that of the New Testament. For example, the Israelites were a type of the New Testament Church. The Old Testament High Priest was a type of the New Testament Pastor. The Old Testament Prophet was a type of the New Testament Prophet. In like manner the Old Testament King was a type of the New Testament Apostle.

In light of this, we see a wonderful example of the Apostolic, in the life of Solomon; especially as this Apostolic anointing is released in the construction of the temple. In 2 Chronicles 5: 1–14, we see a beautiful picture of what could happen when the Apostolic anointing is fully restored to the Church.

"So all the work that Solomon had done for the house of the Lord was finished; and Solomon brought in the things *which his father David had dedicated*: the silver and the gold and all the furnishings. And he put them in the treasuries of the house of God. "Now Solomon *assembled the elders of Israel and all the heads of the tribes, the chief fathers of the children of Israel,* in Jerusalem, that they might bring the Ark of the Covenant of the Lord up from the City of David, which is Zion. Therefore all the men of Israel assembled with the king at the feast, which was in the seventh month. So *all the elders of Israel* came, and the Levites took up the ark. Then they brought up the ark, the tabernacle of meeting, and all the holy furnishings that were in the tabernacle.

The priests and the Levites brought them up. Also King Solomon, and all the congregation of Israel, who were assembled with him before the ark, were sacrificing sheep and oxen that could not be counted or numbered for multitude. Then the priests brought in the ark of the covenant of the Lord to its place, into the inner sanctuary of the temple, to the Most Holy Place, under the wings of the cherubim. For the cherubim spread their wings over the place of the ark, and the cherubim overshadowed the ark and its poles. The poles extended so that the ends of the poles of the ark could be seen from the holy place, in front of the inner sanctuary; but they could not be seen from outside. And they are there to this day. *Nothing was in the ark except the two tablets*, which Moses put there at Horeb, when the Lord made a covenant with the children of Israel, when they had come out of Egypt. And it came to pass when the priests came out of the Most Holy Place (*for all the priests who were present had sanctified themselves, without keeping to their divisions*), and the Levites who were the singers, all those of Asaph and Heman and Jeduthun, with their sons and their brethren, stood at the east end of the altar, clothed in white linen, having cymbals, stringed instruments and harps, and with them one hundred and twenty priests sounding with trumpets – Indeed it came to pass, when the trumpeters and singers *were as one*, to make one sound to be heard in praising and thanking the Lord, and when they lifted up their voice with the trumpets and cymbals and instruments of music, and praised the Lord, saying: *'For He is good, For His mercy endures forever,'* That the house, the house of the Lord, was filled with a cloud, so that the priests could not continue ministering because of the cloud; for the glory of the Lord filled the house of God." 2 Chronicles 5:1-14 (Italics added)

There are several powerful truths that we need to explore from this awesome account:

"Which his father David had dedicated" - As was previously stated, Solomon represents a type of the Apostolic, and we need to understand that David represents the previous move of God, which was the restoration of Prophets to His Church.

Solomon recognized and used that which David dedicated to the building of the house of God. Apostles need Prophets. The house of God, the Church, cannot be built in this hour without what has gone before. We are not experiencing a "new reformation" as some think, we are continuing the reformation that was started in 1501. We cannot, in this hour, throw away what was left us by the previous moves of God; this is very vital. I see in some camps that they are trying to "reinvent the wheel." This is folly. We need to use what the Lord has already provided for us, and build with it, in addition to any new revelation given.

I see some groups trying to take "credit" for the move of God in this hour, but let me re-emphasize. What we are seeing and experiencing today, stems from what has gone before. It is a progressive work of the Holy Spirit. The Word of God declares a powerful truth in the following verse:

"Then He said to them, "Therefore every scribe instructed concerning the kingdom of heaven is like a householder who brings out of his treasure things *new and old.*" Matthew 13:52 (Italics added)

We must always remember that there is a dimension to the foundation of the Church of Jesus Christ, which cannot be improved upon, and that is what was laid by the early Apostles,

Jesus Christ, Himself being the "*Chief Cornerstone*".

As with every building, there are various levels or dimensions of foundations: There is the main foundation, from which the building gets its size, shape and height (that foundation has already been laid and cannot be re-laid by anyone living today)! There are also substructures with its accompanying foundations, for example the walls that have their foundation in the pillars; windows have lintels; the roof have beams as its foundation.

Paul declares:

> "For we are God's fellow workers; you are God's field, you are God's building. According to the grace of God, which was given to me, as a wise master builder I have laid the foundation and another builds upon it. But let everyone take heed how he builds on it. *For no other foundation can anyone lay than that which is laid, which is Jesus Christ*". 1 Corinthians 3: 9-11 (Italics added)

There are some Apostolic camps today, that are trying to re-lay the original foundation, and this **cannot** happen. As was said before, the main foundation of the church has already been laid, and cannot be re-laid, because the main foundation of the Church *is, and I say is, Jesus Christ, Himself*! What a liberating truth! Some men will die, trying to re-lay the foundations of the Church, because it is an exercise in futility. Hear me - "*the main foundation of the Church has already been laid, and it is Jesus Christ*". However there are many local churches and denominations that are built on foundations of error, and these need to be destroyed and rebuilt, on the true foundation of the revelation of Jesus Christ, and this is the function of the Apostles and Prophets.

I encourage you therefore to receive the Apostolic restoration, and allow the Spirit of the Lord to use the Apostolic gift, to bring divine order and government to the Church of Jesus Christ. What I believe is taking place in this hour, is that the Holy Spirit has released the authority for Apostles to lay the foundation for the roof of God's building, the Church. In architecture, there are several foundations in a building: There is the main foundation, which is constructed under the earth, but there are foundations for the construction of walls, windows, attic, roof, etc as was highlighted before.

The Church of Jesus Christ has made tremendous strides over the last two thousand years, and we have arrived at the stage for the "roof" of the building to be put on. However, before doing this, the foundation to hold the "roof" must be laid, and this I believe is now taking place with the restoration of Apostles.

If we have to go back to the original foundations in this hour, then what we are saying is, that which was laid by Jesus Christ and the early Apostles and Prophets was inaccurate, and this is not true. We are also saying, that the work that was done through all the mighty men of God, down through the centuries, has become null and void, and this is also untrue. Even through the "Dark Ages" the Church of Jesus Christ was being built, and this was evidenced by the fact that in 1501 Martin Luther heard the voice of the Lord and responded, bringing forth what is known as the great reformation, which continues to this very day – albeit in different stages!

Again let me re-emphasize. The present reformation is not detached from all that has gone before. It is a continuation of what started with Martin Luther, and just as he did not re-lay the main foundations, but built upon it, we are not to attempt relaying the original foundations, but build upon it and establish the foundations for the "roof" to be placed on God's building.

A further look at the Apostolic example in Solomon will reveal the following:

He assembled the elders of Israel and all the heads of the tribes, the chief fathers of the children of Israel. The Apostolic has the anointing to bring God ordained leadership together. This is one of the critical things that will be established as the Apostles are restored to the Church. We will see several different camps coming together for the glory of God. However, we need to understand that for this to be accomplished, it will cost us. This will not take place without deliberate action. It is very important to note where the temple was built, and where the elders and leaders were gathered.

"Now Solomon began to build the house of the Lord at Jerusalem on Mount Moria, where the Lord had appeared to his father David, at the place that David had prepared on *the threshing floor of Ornan the Jebusite.*"   2 Chronicles 3:1 (Italics added)

The Threshing Floor Of Ornan The Jebusite

"Now satan stood up against Israel, and moved David to number Israel... And God was displeased with this thing; therefore He struck Israel... Therefore, the angel of the Lord commanded Gad to say to David that David should go and *erect an altar* to the Lord on *the threshing floor of Ornan the Jebusite.* So David went up at the word of Gad, which he had spoken in the name of the Lord. Now Ornan turned and saw the angel; and his four sons who were with him hid themselves, but Ornan continued threshing wheat. So David came to Ornan, and Ornan looked and saw David. And he went out from the threshing floor, and bowed before David with his face to the ground. Then David said to Ornan, 'Grant me the place of this threshing floor, that I may build an altar on it to the Lord. You shall grant it to me *at the full price*, for I will not take what is yours for the Lord, nor offer burnt offerings with that *which costs me nothing.*' So David gave Ornan six hundred shekels of gold by weight for the place. And David built there an altar to the Lord, and offered burnt offerings, and called on the Lord; and He answered him from heaven by fire on the altar of burnt offering. So the Lord commanded the angel, and he returned his sword to its sheath. At that time, when David saw that the Lord had answered him on *the threshing floor of Ornan the Jebusite*, he sacrificed there." 1 Chronicles 21:1,7,18-28 (Italics added)

In order for the Apostolic to unite God-ordained leadership in this hour, the competitive spirit must be laid aside. We must not judge our strength and authority by the size of our congregation or networks.

He then brought the Ark of the Covenant of the Lord to its place in the inner sanctuary. However, the contents of the Ark were very important, so there must be a full understanding of the issues surrounding the contents of the Ark.

Issues Of The Contents Of The Ark

♦ **The missing golden pot of manna**. A very strange and puzzling statement is made.

"Nothing was in the ark except the two tablets which Moses put there at Horeb, when the Lord made a covenant with the children of Israel, when they had come out of Egypt". 2 Chronicles 5:10

However, the Ark of the Covenant contained more than just the two tablets of the law. A closer look at the book of Hebrews will reveal this:

"Then indeed, even the first covenant had ordinances of divine service and the earthly sanctuary. For a tabernacle was prepared was prepared; the first part, in which was the lampstand, the table, and the showbread, which is called the sanctuary; and behind the second veil, the part of the tabernacle which is called the Holiest of All, which had the golden censer and the ark of the covenant overlaid on all sides with gold, in which were *the golden pot of manna, Aaron's rod that budded, and the tablets of the covenant;*" Hebrews 9: 1-4 (Italics added)

Manna represented a type of the revelation of God, (Matthew 4:4) that was given to deal with the issue of murmuring, (Exodus 16:1-13, 32). Murmuring against God-ordained leadership must cease, for the glory of God to manifest. Part of the technology of the Apostolic gift, is the wisdom to decode the mysteries of God and release it to the Church. This will give the people of God a constant supply of fresh truth, so the murmuring and frustration will cease. This is why there must be a full acceptance of the restoration of Apostles in this hour.

The Ark of the Covenant did not contain the manna, when the glory of God manifested in Solomon's temple, because it was hidden in Christ. Jesus is the true manna, (John 6:30-59) but to partake of this manna, that has been hidden from ages and generations, we must be *"Overcomers"*:

"He who has an ear, let him hear what the Spirit says to

the churches. To him who *overcomes* I will give some of the *hidden manna to eat*. And I will give him a white stone, and on the stone a new name written which no one knows except him who receives it.'" Revelation 2:17 (Italics added)

I prophetically declare to you that the Apostolic has the grace and the release from God to take the church into the "*overcoming*" dimension.

♦ **This was a type of God's authority**. Aaron's rod resulted because of murmuring, fighting for position and struggle for authority among the Israelites, (Numbers 16: 1-35). God then settled the matter in the following way:

"And the Lord spoke to Moses, saying; 'Speak to the children of Israel, and get from them a rod from each father's house, all their leaders according to their fathers' houses – twelve rods. Write each man's name on his rod. 'And you shall write Aaron's name on the rod of Levi. For there shall be one rod for the head of each father's house. 'Then you shall place them in the tabernacle of meeting before the Testimony, where I meet with you. 'And it shall be that *the rod of the man whom I choose will blossom; thus I will rid Myself of the complaints of the children of Israel*, which they make against you.' So Moses spoke to the children of Israel, and each of their leaders gave him a rod apiece, for each leader according to their fathers' houses, twelve rods; and the rod of Aaron was among their rods. And Moses placed the rods before the Lord in the tabernacle of witness. Now it came to pass on the next day that Moses went into the tabernacle of witness, and behold, *the rod of Aaron, of the house of*

Levi, had sprouted and put forth buds, had produced blossoms and yielded ripe almonds. Then Moses brought out all the rods from before the Lord to all the children of Israel; and they looked, and each man took his rod. And the Lord said to Moses, *'Bring Aaron's rod back before the Testimony, to be kept as a sign against the rebels,* that you may put their complaints away from Me, lest they die.'" Numbers 17:1-10 (Italics added)

The Ark of the Covenant did not contain Aaron's rod when the glory of God manifested in Solomon's temple, because it was hidden in Christ. All authority is now in Christ and has been delegated to the Church by Him, (Matthew 28:18). The glory of God will always be manifested in any place that Jesus Christ is truly Lord, where God-ordained leadership and divine revelation is present.

As the Apostles are restored, the Five-Fold ministry will be complete, and the church will be in a place for the glory of God to be manifested.

God hid the revelation of Himself and the issues of authority in Christ. Jesus was declared to be the true manna that came down from heaven - John 6: 22-65 (another issue of murmuring again) and Revelation 2:17

Jesus promises us that all issues of authority are now in Him. All we need to do is overcome the world, the flesh and the devil, and it's ours. Let us just take a look at some of the promises that the Lord makes for those who overcome:

"He who has an ear let him hear what the Spirit says to the churches. To him who *overcomes* I will give to eat from the tree of life, which is in the midst of the Paradise of God." Revelation 2:7 (Italics added)

"He who has an ear, let him hear what the Spirit says to the churches. To him who *overcomes* I will give some of *hidden manna* to eat. And I will give him a white stone, and on the stone a new name written which no one knows except him who receives it." Revelation 2:17 (Italics added)

"And he who *overcomes*, and keeps My works until the end, to him I will give *power over the nations*-'He shall rule them with a rod of iron; They shall be dashed to pieces like the potter's vessels.'- as I also have received from My Father; 'and I will give him the morning star. He who has an ear, let him hear what the Spirit says to the churches.'" Revelation 2: 26-29 (Italics added)

"He who *overcomes*, I will make him a pillar in the temple of My God, and he shall go out no more. I will write on him the name of My God and the name of the city of My God, the New Jerusalem, which comes down out of heaven from My God. And I will write on him My new name. He who has an ear, let him hear what the Spirit says to the churches." Revelation 3:12-13 (Italics added)

"To him who *overcomes* I will grant to sit with Me on My throne, *as I also overcame* and sat down with My Father on His throne. He who has an ear, let him hear what the Spirit says to the churches." Revelation 3:21-22 (Italics added)

At that time the tablets of the law were the only things present in the Ark. The two tablets of the law represented the moral code by which the children of Israel lived. They were not removed because they were to act as our schoolmaster until Christ:

"Therefore the law was our tutor to bring us to Christ, that we might be justified by faith. But after faith has come, we are no longer under a tutor." Galatians 3:24

The law is what keeps this world from total decay and chaos; it is the moral agent that convicts people's hearts, thus allowing the Holy Spirit to draw them to Christ.

So as we move deeper into the Apostolic restoration, greater strength for overcoming is being released in the Church. As the Apostles are fully restored; the Church will grow into the fullness of the measure of the stature of Christ, unto a perfect man (Ephesians 4:11-13). This is the most glorious time to be alive, as the Church of Jesus Christ is coming into full maturity. We will see the demonstration of the power and glory of God in this season, such as we have never experienced before.

With the Apostles restored, along with the Prophets, Evangelists, Pastors and Teachers, the saints will be thoroughly equipped to do the works of the ministry. I declare to you that the glory of God will cover this earth as the waters cover the sea!

Chapter Six
Pillar Four - Wealth

And with great power the Apostles gave witness to the resurrection of the Lord Jesus. And great grace was upon them all. Nor was there anyone among them who lacked; for all who were possessors of lands or houses sold them, and brought the proceeds of the things that were sold, And laid them at the Apostles' feet; and they distributed to each as anyone had need. And Joses, who was also named Barnabas by the Apostles (which is translated Son of Encouragement), a Levite of the country of Cyrus, Having land, sold it, and brought the money and laid it at the Apostles' feet." Acts 4:33-37

As we move deeper into the restoration of Apostles, the restoration of wealth back to the house of God will become very evident. At the beginning of the Church, in the book of Acts, we read that money was brought and laid at the feet of the early Apostles, and they distributed it as they saw fit.

Please note that the wealth that was laid at the Apostles' feet was for distribution and not for them. The Apostolic has a grace gift to attract wealth to fulfill its God-given mandate.

Wealth has always been a turning point for most churches, either for good or for bad, but with the restoration of the Apostles, God will release greater clarity on how to manage wealth.

As was earlier said, the kings of the Old Testament paralleled the Apostles of the New Testament, so it will be worthwhile to go back to the rules and guidelines that were set down by God, for the establishment of kings.

Long before Israel had a king, God had laid down a set of principles for their function. This can be found in the book of Deuteronomy:

"When you come to the land which the Lord your God is giving you, and possess it and dwell in it, and say, 'I will set a king over me like all the nations that are around me,' you shall surely set a king over you whom the Lord your God chooses; one from among your brethren you shall set as king over you; you may not set a foreigner over you, who is not your brother. But *he shall not multiply horses for himself, nor cause the people to return to Egypt to multiply horses*, for the Lord has said to you, 'You shall not return that way again.' 'Neither shall he multiply wives for himself, lest his heart turn away; *nor shall he greatly multiply silver and gold for himself.* Also it shall be, when he sits on the throne of his kingdom, that he shall write for himself a copy of this law in a book, from the one before the priests, the Levites. And it shall be with him, and he shall read it all the days of his life, that he may learn to fear the Lord his God and be careful to observe all the words of this law and these statutes, that his heart may not be lifted above his brethren, that he may not turn aside from the commandment to the right hand or to the left, and that he may prolong his days in

his kingdom, he and his children in the midst of Israel.'"
Deuteronomy 17:14-20 (Italics added)

From this passage several principles can be gleaned, but
let's concentrate on what is relevant to this chapter on
"*Apostolic wealth*".

Please understand that these principles and guidelines were
given long before Israel had a king. One of the things of major
concern to the Lord was the issue of wealth.

**The Lord gave specific instructions concerning wealth
for the king:**

    a. **he shall not multiply horses for himself** (verse 16),
this spoke about military might in the natural. The
king's military was not to be in his accumulation of
military hardware, but in the Lord.

    b. **nor shall he greatly multiply silver and gold for
himself** (verse 17b). This is very clear. The king
was not to use his position to multiply wealth for
himself. It is similar with the Apostles today.
Apostles must not use their anointing and position to
build up a financial empire for themselves.
However, it is important to note that there is an
anointing for wealth upon the Apostolic, but that
should never be the primary focus as some will want
to make it.

    c. **nor cause the people to return to Egypt to
multiply horses** (verse 16b). This is very
interesting and carries with it the following
understanding - the kings were not to draw their
substance from the world or from the pagan systems

that existed in their day. In like manner Apostles of today must not rely on the world's system to acquire wealth or warfare technology to advance the kingdom of God. They must rely on the supernatural hand of provision that the Lord gives.

This was in direct contrast to Saul, because he broke the commandments that were laid down by the Lord regarding the king's office. (1 Samuel 8:11-19; 1 Samuel 15:1-9)

Discernment will be a key element in these last days as the Lord restores His Apostles back to His Church, as there will be false Apostles who will draw wealth unto themselves and not primarily to further God's kingdom in the earth.

These principles are very important as we look at the whole issue of wealth as a pillar of the Apostolic.

The Wealth Transfer

Another powerful scripture that will be fulfilled in this season of Apostolic restoration is Proverbs 13:22b

"But the wealth of the sinner is stored up for the righteous."

Please note that the word of God declares that wealth is stored up for the *righteous*, and not just the Christian. The righteous spoken of here, are the saints who do not compromise the word of God, who are willing to obey God at His word. However, this wealth is stored up somewhere, and as such, there must be what we call a wealth transfer. In Isaiah 45:1-3 (Emphasis added) the Lord declares:

"Thus says the Lord to His anointed, To Cyrus, whose

right hand I have held – To subdue nations before him
And loose the armour of kings, To open before him the
double doors, So that the gates will not be shut: 'I will go
before you And make the crooked places straight; I will
break in pieces the gates of bronze And cut the bars of
iron. *I will give you the treasures of darkness And hidden
riches of secret places,* That you may know that I, the
Lord, Who call you by your name, Am the God of
Israel." (Italics added)

The treasures and riches are hidden and in this hour the Lord
is beginning to uncover them to His holy Apostles and
Prophets. We are going to see tremendous sums of wealth
transferred into the treasuries of the righteous. One of the main
avenues of this transfer is through the avenue of business.

This Brings Us To The Issue Of Kingdom Business!

* What Is A Kingdom Business?

Every so often we need to re-define things in order that they
may remain relevant. One thing that is being re-defined with
the restoration of Apostles is *"Christian Business."*

What does it mean to be a Christian businessman or
woman? Why should a Christian own a business? What is
kingdom business? A proper understanding of the subject is
needed, if we are going to position ourselves to receive the
promises God made to us, about wealth transfer and the
acquiring of treasure that is hidden in secret places.

In exploring this, one of the very first things that we need to
understand, is the fact that Almighty God has made a covenant
to bless His people, in order that His Kingdom could advance.
Deuteronomy 8:18 states:

"And you shall remember the Lord your God, *for it is He who gives you power to get wealth, that He may establish His covenant* which He swore to your fathers, as it is this day." (Italics added)

From this passage of scripture we can learn several things. One is the fact that God confirms the Abrahamic covenant to the seed of Abraham with prosperity. As the children of Abraham through faith, we step into this heritage. There are so many scriptures that confirm God's promise to prosper His people. So the first point is that a kingdom businessperson must have their faith secure in these promises for prosperity.

You must believe that God is with you, and for you, because He wants to make good on His word. Secondly, it says in that verse, that God gives us the power to get wealth. The first step to receiving power, or ability from God to obtain or acquire wealth, is to have vision for the wealth. The same amount of wealth that existed on the earth from its creation is still on the earth today. It has only changed its form or switched hands over time, but it is still on the earth.

You need to have a vision that includes a strategy to transfer some of that wealth out of the hands of the wicked, and into the hands of the righteous (*the Church*). As a "Kingdom businessman or woman, you can't be satisfied to be in business, just to be in business. You need a large enough vision that would turn God on, to give you the ability to achieve your goals. You need to know where the wealth is located (which market) and come up with a strategy to transfer that wealth.

Isaac knew where to dig for water. I fear that too many believers enter business without clear direction as to what resource they are trying to tap. They end up doing something in business that they see others doing. They have not studied the market to see where the money is. They limit themselves to their present ability, and settle down in their comfort zones, while God is waiting for them to make a move, so that He can transfer wealth into their hands.

Don't let your present ability limit your vision. You must know where the resources of wealth are in the earth, and devise a plan or strategy to obtain it. God is going to help you in that. But if you just want to be in business for some other reason without having a vision to transfer the wealth in the earth from the wrong hands into the right hands, you are not going to trigger God's blessing in any major way.

Jesus said in relation to money, that, "the sons of this world are more wise in their generation, than the sons of light." He was observing something that is a tendency with God's people. They tend to rely on God so much, that they don't put forth enough effort in obtaining something. God is with us to give us the wisdom and the ability to get wealth, but we must apply ourselves.

Some Christians in business have unrealistic dreams about God blessing their business, regardless of how non-strategically their businesses are set up to transfer the wealth of the world into their hands. Christians rely too much on God for miracles, and too little on Him who works with us, as we apply ourselves and put forth effort. How convenient! They end up surviving and giving testimony to the God, who always provides what they need. That's great, but it's not the standard for a kingdom business.

Please understand that wealth is always being transferred from one place to the next, for certain periods of time. As a result "Kingdom Businesses" need to recognize certain shifts in the market, and move with it. Your power to get wealth is only as good as your vision or your ability to see where the wealth is. Are you in business to obtain wealth? Or are you in it because it's better than working for someone else? Are you in it just to afford a comfortable lifestyle? If you are in the last two categories, you simply cannot expect real wealth for the kingdom. You can expect whatever your vision allows. So do you have a kingdom position for the vision of your business?

Based then on the aforesaid, here are some factors that defines a "Kingdom Business"

Mentality Of The Kingdom

Kingdom businesses must be linked to a larger Apostolic paradigm and Apostolic purpose or mentality. The ethos, and culture of the business, must reflect Apostolic trends such as creativity, discipline, faith, breakthrough, prosperity, success, global mentality and networking.

Investing Accurately

It would be a shame for an entrepreneur who is a believer, with the God-given ability for reaping great financial harvests, to invest inaccurately in the kingdom of God, particularly when it is this very same God who has blessed him with those finances. This would be a waste, because that entrepreneur would have missed the purpose for which God blessed him with those finances. It would qualify that believer as an unwise steward of the Master's resources.

There are many works in the world today that qualify as "*good works*," both in the secular world as well as in the church world. You could actually give finances into any of these good works, and be doing well. But the issue is not about throwing money into the realm of good works. Rather, it is one of investing in those particular projects that are foremost on the mind and heart of God, for the *Now*! Every one who invests in the stock market understands the importance of timings and seasons and trends and demands.

There is a wise time to buy and a wise time to sell, which is usually, determined by market trends and product demands. Investing accurately is absolutely related to timing. It is the same with investing in the kingdom of God. As God unfolds His kingdom advancement strategies, we should invest accordingly. In I Chronicles 12:32 it is stated that the sons of Issachar had understanding of the times, and therefore knew what Israel ought to do. Doing the right or accurate thing depends on understanding the times. Investing into kingdom works, also depends on discerning the times and seasons of the Lord. If you invest religiously, because it is the right thing to do, then you will still not be investing properly into the kingdom of God.

Many believers are not aware that God is building something very strategically, and deliberately, according to ancient plans, which mean that at present, the kingdom-building project is in a certain phase, with specific needs and emphases and operations unlike any other time. There is a present kingdom product in demand, by God's timetable. There are present needs that are new and different from those of yesteryear. If you simply give to be doing something good, without understanding the kingdom demands, the kingdom market trends, the kingdom timings and seasons, you will invest inaccurately. If you give to churches that are not building according to the timings and seasons of the Lord, but are involved in traditional religious activities, you will invest inaccurately.

Accuracy in the area of kingdom activity is totally dependent on a proper discerning of the times. The times reveal to us where God is currently active in advancing His Kingdom. Jesus said he would only do what he was seeing the Father do, not what he saw the Father do at some former period. Many financial investments end up in works that God is no longer emphasizing. God has moved on, and man must constantly discern His migration and move with Him, in order to be spiritually accurate. You have to become a Prophetic believer to know where God is currently building. You need to develop an ability to hear God and to receive revelation truth.

A great example could be found in the context of the early church. When the Apostles were teaching new revelation in the midst of an old and well-established religious center, people had to choose between the two, and commit to the right one, in order to be accurate. If believers at that time continued to sow their finances in the old Jewish Temple, and not in the new Apostolic church, they would have been investing wrongly. They could not know the difference apart from a Prophetic ear, or an ability to understand truth non-traditionally.

Giving into traditional religious good works is not investing accurately in God's kingdom. It might still accomplish some earthly good, and it might still earn you some points in the records of heaven, but it will not advance the invasion of God's kingdom on the planet in the present season. It will not be supporting His eternal purpose for the present. God's kingdom advancement on the earth can only be funded by a people who can discern the timings of God.

Kingdom accuracy is not equal to every good, religious, well-established work. There are a lot of religious works that have built worldly kingdoms, instead of a house, for God to dwell in. Not everything we see with our physical eyes that look like church is in fact church according to God's design. The need for discernment in these last days, to know the true church and the current speaking and workings of God, is great. Ecclesiastes Chapter Three is a worthy passage to meditate on, to appreciate the value and importance of understanding the times, in relation to doing things. Verse 17 (b) says; ".... there is a time there for every purpose and for every work." Accuracy in kingdom investment is in knowing what God is doing at the present time.[2]

Babylon Will Be Judged

Babylon is a demonic system in the earth set up by the devil. This system controls most of the kings of the earth, commerce and trade and is very anti-Christ.

"Then one of the seven angels who had the seven bowls came and talked with me, saying to me, "Come, I will show you the judgement of the great harlot who sits on many waters, "with whom *the kings of the earth* committed fornication, and the inhabitants of the earth were made drunk with the wine of her fornication." So he carried me away in the Spirit into the wilderness. And I saw a woman sitting on a scarlet beast which was *full of names of blasphemy*, having seven heads and ten horns. The woman was arrayed in purple and scarlet, and adorned with gold and precious stones and pearls, having in her hand a golden cup full of abominations and the filthiness of her fornication. And on her forehead a name was written: MYSTERY, BABYLON THE GREAT, THE MOTHER OF HARLOTS AND OF THE ABOMINATIONS OF THE EARTH.

---

[2] (* This section is an extract from an article written by Snr. Elder Eric Vlaugh of Acts 29 Caribbean Resource Center and International Ministries in St Maarten, N.A)

I saw the woman drunk with the *blood of the saints and with blood of the martyrs of Jesus*. And when I saw her, I marvelled with great amazement." Revelation 17: 1-6 (Italics added)

At this current time Babylon still controls the wealth of the earth and has been mandated by the devil to destroy the Apostolic and Prophetic. They know that once these two ministry gifts are fully restored to the Church, their kingdom is coming down. As a matter of fact the Lord has already given us the script – Babylon is going to fall and a decree will be issued in the heavens, and the Apostles and Prophets are to rejoice at her demise:

"They threw dust on their heads and cried out, weeping and wailing, and saying, 'Alas, alas, that great city, in which all who had ships on the sea became rich by her wealth! For in one hour she is made desolate.' *"Rejoice over her, O heaven, and you holy apostles and prophets*, for God has avenged you on her!" Revelation 18:19-20 (Italics added)

This is why there is a clarion call going out in the Spirit, through the Apostles and Prophets to all of God's people who are still trapped in Babylon, to come out of her. There are many, because of lack of understanding, which are trapped in Babylon. However, in this hour God is releasing the wisdom and revelation through His holy Apostles to draw them out of Babylon.

"And I heard another voice from heaven saying, *"Come out of her, my people*, lest you share in her sins, and lest you receive of her plagues. "For her sins have reached to heaven, and God has remembered her iniquities." Revelation 18:4-5 (Italics added)

I submit to you, that as soon as those who belong to the Lord come out of Babylon, it will signal the end of that polluted system. They will be used of the Lord, to effect a large portion of the wealth transfer.

It will be similar to what happened to the Egyptians when the Israelites left. Only this time, the effects will be far more devastating.

In the book of Genesis there is an account of an incredible incident that took place when the Israelites were about to depart from Egypt.

"And the Lord said to Moses, "I will bring one more plague on Pharaoh and on Egypt. Afterward he will let you go from here. When he lets you go, he will surely drive you out of here altogether. "Speak now in the hearing of the people, and let every man ask from his neighbour and every woman from her neighbour, articles of silver and articles of gold." Exodus 11:1-2

"And the Egyptians urged the people, that they might send them out of the land in haste. For they said, "We shall all be dead." So the people took their dough before it was leavened, having their kneading bowls bound up in their clothes on their shoulders. Now the children of Israel had done according to the word of Moses, and they had asked from the Egyptians articles of silver, articles of gold, and clothing. And the Lord had given the people favour in the sight of the Egyptians, so that they granted them what they requested. *Thus they plundered the Egyptians.*" Exodus 12:31-36 (Italics added)

That was incredible. Imagine the Egyptians actually giving the Israelites their wealth? Talk about the wealth of the sinner being laid up for the righteous. The favour of the Lord accomplished it.

The Lord is releasing this same favour as He calls His people out of Babylon. If you are called to be a kingdom businessman or woman today, this is the time to dismantle any or all of Babylon's structure and spirit that may exist in your business.

However, in the midst of the wealth transfer that is taking place, and will continue to take place as the Apostles are fully accepted into the Church, there is a caution.

Let us resist any temptation to do as the Israelites did and build a golden calf with this wealth. As it happened, the Israelites made wealth their god. (Exodus 32)

As with every move of God, there are going to be excesses and falsity and certain ones will make money their god, thereby setting him or herself up to become like fallen Babylon, a dwelling place for demons:

"And he cried mightily with a loud voice, saying, *"Babylon the great is fallen, is fallen, and has become a dwelling place of demons*, a prison for every foul spirit, and a cage for every unclean and hated bird!" Revelation 18:2 (Italics added)

I want to conclude this chapter with the admonition from Timothy:

"If anyone teaches otherwise and does not consent to wholesome words, even the word of our Lord Jesus Christ, and to the doctrine which accords with godliness, he is proud, knowing nothing, but is obsessed with disputes and arguments over words, from which come envy, strife, reviling, evil suspicions, useless wranglings of men of corrupt minds and destitute of the truth, who suppose that godliness is a means of gain. From such withdraw yourself. Now godliness with contentment is great gain. For we brought nothing into this world, and it is certain we can carry nothing out. And having food and clothing, with these we shall be content. But those who desire to be rich fall into temptation and a snare, and into many foolish and harmful lusts which drown men in destruction. For the *love of money is a root of all kinds of evil*, for which some have strayed from the faith in their greediness, and pierced themselves through with many sorrows." 1 Timothy 6:3-10 (Italics added)

Chapter Seven
Pillar Five
Miracles, Signs & Wonders

L ater He appeared to the eleven [Apostles] as they sat at the table; and He rebuked their unbelief and hardness of heart, because they did not believe those who had seen Him after He had risen. And He said to them, 'Go into all the world and preach the gospel to every creature. 'He who believes and is baptized will be saved; but he who does not believe will be condemned. 'And these signs will follow those who believe: In My name they will cast out demons; they will speak with new tongues; 'they will take up serpents; and if they drink anything deadly, it will by no means hurt them; they will lay hands on the sick, and they will recover.' So then, after the Lord had spoken to them, He was received up into heaven, and sat down at the right hand of God. And they went out and preached everywhere, the Lord working with them and *confirming* the word through the accompanying signs. Amen. Mark 16:19-20 (Italics and Parenthesis added)

This passage of scripture is what is known as the "*Great Commission*". It can also be referred to, as the Apostolic Mandate that was given to the early Apostles, by Jesus Himself.

Primarily, the Church began with the commissioning of the Apostles to go into the entire world, and preach the gospel, with signs, wonders and miracles following. It is important to note here, that the Lord will only confirm that which has been sent forth in the "Apostolic spirit". This is why Apostles are part of the foundation upon which the church is built.

Most people in reading Mark 16 and Matthew 28 immediately see the Evangelist at work, in what is referred to as the "*Great Commission*". However, as we look at this scripture, we see that it was the mandate given to the Apostles.

Let me make this clear, Evangelists are needed in fulfilling the "*Great Commission*", but to be truly effective; they must function from an Apostolic foundation. In fact, in these last days, we will see more of an Apostolic/Evangelistic spirit being released upon the saints of the Most High, in order for the great end-time harvest to be accomplished.

As true Apostles are restored, and become fully functional and accepted in the Church, then we will see an awesome display of Apostolic miracles, signs and wonders, through which God will confirm the genuine call of an Apostle. This will also result in a mighty harvest of souls into the Kingdom of God.

The Body of Christ will be incomplete, without fully functioning Apostles in it. Let me once again re-emphasize the fact of Ephesians 4:11-16: Apostles are needed in order to assist with the equipping of the saints, that we might become mature and do the works of the ministry, which includes miracles, signs and wonders.

A devious lie has been perpetrated by the devil in the Body of Christ, and sad to say, there are many who still believe that lie, which is to say that miracles, signs and wonders are no longer evident, as they ceased with the original eleven Apostles and the Apostle Paul. This one lie did two things:

1. It destroyed faith in the saints, and consequently the operation God's miraculous power.

2. It destroyed faith in the Apostle's ministry.

While no Apostle will ever hold the position of the 12, including the Apostle Paul (1 Corinthians 15:3-11), it does not mean they were the only New Testament Apostles, and that the gift should die and no longer be in use, as recorded in the Book of Acts. If you do away with the Apostle's ministry as defined in the New Testament, then you also do away with the *Power of God in the signs* of an Apostle.

"Truly the signs of an Apostle were accomplished among you with all perseverance, in signs and wonders and mighty deeds." 2 Corinthians 12:12

When we reject the ministry gift of an Apostle as defined in the Bible, then we are resisting and fighting against the signs of an Apostle in signs and wonders and mighty deeds. It is impossible to have the fullness of the miraculous power of God present in this generation, without the full acceptance of the chosen vessels, sent to bring this Apostolic anointing. When we reject the truth, we are rejecting God's power to save souls in this generation.

Meaning And Origin Of Miracle

The word miracle in English comes from the Latin word "*miraculum*", which means something, amazing, astonishing, extraordinary, and not explainable by natural means. Miracles are distinguished from natural events, which are constant and predictable, because miracles are out of the natural order, out of ordinary happenings.

Greek Word For Miracle

The Greek word most used by the New Testament, as miracle is "*semeion*", which is found 77 times, 13 of them in Matthew, 7 in Mark, 10 in Luke and 17 in John. Another Greek word used in the New Testament is "*teras*", which means wonder, like for instance when Jesus said that the false Christs show signs and wonders to deceive (Mark 13:22; Matthew 24:24). Related to the word miracle is the Greek verb "*thaumazo*", which is found 43 times in the New Testament and means to be amazed, astonished, as when we read that all marvelled about Jesus, because He cast out the demons at Gadara (Mark 5:20).

Synonyms Of The Word Miracle

The New Testament uses other words as synonyms or equivalent to the word miracle; it also calls it sign or signal, in the sense that a miracle is a signal of something divine. It also uses wonder, as we said before, to mean the power behind the miracle; marvel, which represents the amazing side of the event, as happened with the healing of the paralytic: "And they were all amazed, saying: We have seen strange things today" (Luke 5:20). From all the words to express the meaning and supernatural content of a miraculous fact, the best one is miracle.

No one can truly claim to be an Apostle, without the evidence of miracles, signs and wonders accompanying the ministry. However, not everyone displaying this supernatural anointing is an Apostle. Miracles can also be very present in any of the other Five-Fold ministry gifts. However, unlike the other four, miracles, signs and wonders is one of the areas in testing all claims to the Apostolic office.

Please understand that this in itself does not make a person an Apostle, but instead it is a definite sign of anyone who is called to that office.

In the ministry of Jesus, every time He sent out His Apostles they were expected to function in the supernatural. For example:

Matthew 10:1,5a

"And when He had called His twelve disciples to Him, He gave them power over unclean spirits, to cast them out, and to heal all kinds of sickness and all kinds of disease... ...These twelve Jesus sent out and commanded them, saying..."

Mark 3:14-15

"Then He appointed twelve, that they might be with Him and that He might send them out to preach, and to have power to heal sicknesses and to cast out demons."

Luke 9:1-2

"Then He called His twelve disciples together and gave them power and authority over all demons, and to cure diseases. He sent them to preach the kingdom of God and to heal the sick."

Luke 10:1,9,17

"After these things the Lord appointed seventy others also, and sent them two by two before His face into every city and place where He Himself was about to go... ...And heal the sick there, and say to them, 'The kingdom of God has come near to you.'... ...Then the seventy returned with joy, saying, 'Lord, even the demons are subject to us in Your name.'"

Matthew 17:15-20

"And when they had come to the multitude, a man came to Him, kneeling down to Him and saying, 'Lord, have mercy on my son, for he is an epileptic and suffers severely; for he often falls into the fire and often into the water. *So I brought him to Your disciples, but they could not cure him.'   Then Jesus answered and said, 'O faithless and perverse generation, how long shall I be with you? How long shall I bear with you?* Bring him here to Me.' And Jesus rebuked the demon, and it came out of him; and the child was cured from that very hour. Then the disciples came to Jesus privately and said, 'Why could we not cast it out?' So Jesus said to them, 'Because of your unbelief; for assuredly, I say to you, if you have faith as a mustard seed, you say to this mountain, 'Move from here to there,' and it will move; and nothing will be impossible for you." [The implication here is that these Apostles in training were expected to perform miracles]. (Italics and Parenthesis added)

Because this office is now being restored to the Church, there are many who are ascribing to themselves the calling of an

Apostle. However, many of them are unable to validate their position with the evidence of the accompanying signs, wonders and miracles.

An Interesting Event

In the gospel of John, Jesus did something that had far reaching implications. In the process of healing a man that was blind from his mother's womb, Jesus told him to go and wash in the pool of Siloam, and the bible says that the pool of Siloam is translated "*Sent*".

"And He said to him, 'Go wash in the pool of Siloam' (*which is translated, Sent*). So he went and washed, and came back seeing.' " John 9:7 (Italics added)

This word Sent comes from the same root word as Apostle, which is worth looking at. Jesus was making an awesome connection between Apostles and miracles, signs and wonders. In effect Jesus sent this man to an Apostolic source for his healing. Glory to God, Hallelujah!

Let us review the early Church and see, if miracles, signs and wonders were consistent throughout the ministry of the Apostles.

References from the Acts of the Apostles:

The very first "*wonder*" occurred, when the Holy Spirit arrived, and the Apostles spoke in other tongues for the first time. This was the response from the Jewish crowd that was present.

"And there were dwelling in Jerusalem Jews, devout men, from every nation under heaven. And when this sound occurred, the multitude came together, and was confused, because everyone heard them speak in his own language. Then they were all *amazed and marvelled*, saying to one another, 'Look, are not all these who speak Galileans? 'And how is it that we hear, each in our own language in which we were born? ...we hear them speaking in our own tongues the wonderful works of God.' So they were all *amazed* and perplexed, saying to one another, 'What ever could this mean?'" Acts 2:5-8,11b-12 (Italics added).

Another awesome miracle occurred when Peter and John went up to the temple at the hour of prayer:

"Now Peter and John went up together to the temple at the hour of prayer, the ninth hour. And a certain man *lame from his mother's womb* was carried, whom they laid daily at the gate of the temple which is called Beautiful, to ask alms from those who entered the temple; who, seeing Peter and John about to go into the temple, asked for alms. And fixing his eyes on him, with John, Peter said, "Look at us." So he gave them his attention, expecting to receive something from them. *Then Peter said, "Silver and gold I do not have, but what I do have I give you: In the name of Jesus Christ of Nazareth, rise up and walk."* And he took him by the right hand and lifted him up, *and immediately his feet and ankle bones received strength.* So he, leaping up, stood and walked and entered the temple with them--walking, leaping, and praising God. And *all the people saw him walking and praising God.* Then they knew that it was he who sat begging alms at the Beautiful Gate of the temple; and they were filled with wonder and amazement at what had happened to him. Acts 3:1-10 (Italics added)

"Now when they saw the boldness of Peter and John, and perceived that they were uneducated and untrained men, they *marveled*. And they realized that they had been with Jesus. And seeing the man who had been healed standing with them, they could say nothing against it. But when they had commanded them to go aside out of the council, they conferred among themselves, saying, "What shall we do to these men? *For, indeed, that a notable miracle has been done through them is evident to all who dwell in Jerusalem, and we cannot deny it.* But so that it spreads no further among the people, let us severely threaten them, that from now on they speak to no man in this name." And they called them and commanded them not to speak at all nor teach in the name of Jesus. But Peter and John answered and said to them, "Whether it is right in the sight of God to listen to you more than to God, you judge. For we cannot but speak the things which we have seen and heard." So when they had further threatened them, they let them go, finding no way of punishing them, because of the people, since they all glorified God for what had been done. *For the man was over forty years old on whom this miracle of healing had been performed.* Acts 4:13-22 (Italics added)

Acts 5:12

"And through the hands of the Apostles many signs and wonders were done among the people. And they were all with one accord in Solomon's Porch."

The preceding scriptural references were just a few examples of miracles, signs and wonders, which were consistent throughout the ministry of the Apostles. There are several other references to this throughout the book of Acts[3].

---

[3] Acts 8:14-25, 9:32-35, 9:36-42, 16:16-26, 19:11-20, 20:7-12, 28:1-10

Let us also examine Paul's Apostolic grace and how it functioned:

In 2 Corinthians 12: 11-12 Paul was making a defence for his Apostolic call, and made a very notable and significant statement concerning the qualifications of an Apostle.

"I have become a fool in boasting; you have compelled me. For I ought to have been commended by you; for in nothing was I behind the most eminent Apostles, though I am nothing. Truly the *signs of an Apostle* were accomplished among you with all perseverance, *in signs and wonders and mighty deeds.*" (Italics added)

From this passage it will seem that miracles, signs and wonders were very high on Paul's list of evidence to an Apostolic call and function. This had to be so, as he made mention of it in his first letter to the Corinthian church.

"And I, brethren, when I came to you, did not come with excellence of speech or of wisdom declaring to you the testimony of God. For I determined not to know anything among you except Jesus Christ and Him crucified. I was with you in weakness, in fear, and in much trembling. And my speech and my preaching were not with persuasive words of human wisdom, but *in demonstration of the Spirit and of power*, that your faith should not be in the wisdom of men but in the power of God." 1 Corinthians 2:1-5 (Italics added)

This is very vital in the ministry of an Apostle, as the Apostolic is sent first to pioneer and breakthrough into new territory and for new church plants. If the foundation is built on anything other than the revelation of Jesus Christ, confirmed by signs, wonders and miracles, then the foundation will be wrong and the church will be built wrong.

In Acts 5:12-16 we read:

"And through the hands of the Apostles many signs and wonders were done among the people. And they were all with one accord in Solomon's Porch. Yet none of the rest dared join them, but the people esteemed them highly. And believers were increasingly added to the Lord, multitudes of both men and women, so that they brought the sick out into the streets and laid them on beds and couches, that at least the shadow of Peter passing by might fall on some of them. Also a multitude gathered from the surrounding cities to Jerusalem, bringing sick people and those who were tormented by unclean spirits, and they were all healed."

It did not stop there; but we can trace this same activity throughout the book of Acts as was highlighted earlier.

The Lord is setting the stage for one of the greatest harvests this world has ever seen, and Apostolic miracles, signs and wonders will be at the very core of it. When the bible declares in Ephesians 4 11-12 that Jesus gave the *Five-Fold ministry* for the equipping of the saints for the work of the ministry, miracles, signs and wonders are included in the work of the ministry.

I encourage you, if you are called to an Apostolic function, and miracles, signs and wonders are not present in your life and ministry, this is the hour to seek the Lord and believe in faith, for this to begin functioning in and through you.

Chapter Eight
The Apostles and Church Unity!

The Apostles that are being raised up by the Lord in this hour will be used to influence the unity of the faith. When the Church was birthed in the Upper Room about 2000 years ago, unity was a very vital key in its establishment. At the very heart of that unity were the Apostles of the Lamb.

As the Church grew, Evangelists, Pastors and Teachers came alongside the Apostles and Prophets so that the Five-Fold ministry imparted strength into the early Church.

We also saw during the Dark ages, that there was a falling away, and the visible, functional ministry of the entire Five-Fold ministry was lost, ergo, the Church became very separated.

God then began His restorative process, by first re-establishing the fully functioning Teacher, Pastor, Evangelist, Prophet, and now in this hour, He is fully restoring the Apostle. The Church will never be fully functional without the Apostles being fully released and fully functioning. Jesus Himself knew that this had to happen, hence the reason He did what He did as recorded in the scripture text below:

"But to each one of us grace was given according to the measure of Christ's gift. Therefore He says: 'When He ascended on high, He led captivity captive, And gave gifts to men.' (Now this, 'He ascended' – what does it mean but that He also first descended into the lower parts of the earth? He who descended is also the One who ascended far above all the heavens, that He might fill all things.) And He Himself gave some to be *Apostles*, some Prophets, some Evangelists, and some Pastors and Teachers, for the equipping of the saints for the work of ministry, for the edifying of the body of Christ, *till we all come to the unity of the faith and of the knowledge of the Son of God, to a perfect man, to the measure of the stature of the fullness of Christ*; that we should no longer be children, tossed to and fro and carried about with every wind of doctrine, by the trickery of men, in the cunning craftiness of deceitful plotting, But, speaking the truth in love, may grow up in all things into Him who is the head – Christ-From whom the whole body, joined and knit together by what every joint supplies, according to the effective working by which every part does its share, causes growth of the body for the edifying of itself in love." Ephesians 4:7–16 (Italics added)

Points to extract from Ephesians 4:7–16

♦ Jesus Himself gave the ministry gifts of Apostles, Prophets, Evangelists, Pastors and Teachers to men.

♦ These gifts were given to His body the Church.

♦ They were given for several reasons:

a. for equipping the saints in His body

b. to allow the saints to do the work of the ministry

c. for the edifying of the body of Christ

The ministry gifts were to function in the body of Christ for a specific time period, until the following happens:

a. **we all come into the unity of the faith**

b. we all come into the knowledge of the Son of God

c. we all come into a perfect man, to the measure of the stature of the fullness of Christ

d. we are no longer children, tossed to and fro and carried about with every wind of doctrine

e. we speak the truth in love and grow up in all things into Him who is the head, Christ.

Evidently, these things have not yet been fulfilled in the body of Christ; therefore the ministry gifts are still in operation, with specific emphasis conferred upon that of the Apostle.

As we look back at the Israelites (a type of the Church) and their journey to the Promised Land, we can see some striking similarities with what is happening today.

When God called Abram and sent him on a journey, he took Lot with him, and just before Abram entered *Hebron*, separation had to come between himself and Lot, because division stepped in among them:

"*Lot also, who went with Abram*, had flocks and herds and tents. Now the land was not able to support them, that they might dwell together, for their possessions were so great that they could not dwell together. *And there was strife between the herdsmen of Abram's livestock and the herdsmen of Lot's livestock.* The Canaanites and the Perizzites then dwelt in the land. *So Abram said to Lot,* "Please let there be no strife between you and me, and between my herdsmen and your herdsmen; for we are brethren. Is not the whole land before you? *Please separate from me.* If you take the left, then I will go to the right; or, if you go to the right, then I will go to the left." And Lot lifted his eyes and saw all the plain of Jordan, that it was well watered everywhere (before the LORD destroyed Sodom and Gomorrah) like the garden of the LORD, like the land of Egypt as you go toward Zoar. Then Lot chose for himself all the plain of Jordan, and Lot journeyed east. And they separated from each other. Abram dwelt in the land of Canaan, and Lot dwelt in the cities of the plain and pitched his tent even as far as Sodom. But the men of Sodom were exceedingly wicked and sinful against the LORD. *And the LORD said to Abram, after Lot had separated from him*: "Lift your eyes now and look from the place where you are--northward, southward, eastward, and westward; for all the land which you see I give to you and your descendants forever. And I will make your descendants as the dust of the earth; so that if a man could number the dust of the earth, then your descendants also could be numbered. Arise, walk in the land through its length and its width, for I give it to you." *Then Abram moved his tent, and went and dwelt by the terebinth trees of Mamre, which are in Hebron, and built an altar there to the LORD.*" Genesis 13:5-18 (Italics added)

This was very significant because of what *Hebron* represented. Let's look at the word *Hebron* in Hebrew. It is translated - confederacy, from which the noun, confederate is derived and which carries the following meaning - To unite in a confederacy or to be united in a league. So from this we can derive that Hebron represented a place of unity.

Several centuries later, God delivered the children of Israel from Egypt, and took them on a journey to the land promised to Abraham. During the Israelites' wilderness wandering, the twelve spies sent out to report on the land of Canaan explored the region of Hebron. At that time the 'descendants of Anak' populated it (Numbers 13). These twelve spies represented the twelve tribes, and therefore represented the entire nation of Israel. (As we know, Israel was a type of the New Testament Church and their possession of the Promised Land represents us, the Church, coming into our destiny in God upon the earth.) Please keep this in mind, as it will be very significant later on. As they entered the land of promise, *"Hebron"* (the place of peace) was their point of entry and they found *giants* living there. This caused a major split to occur among the twelve. Ten of them brought back an evil report and two, Joshua (a type of the Apostolic) and Caleb (a type of the Prophetic) came back confident that the land could have been taken.

> "Then Caleb quieted the people before Moses, and said, 'Let us go up at once and take possession, for we are well able to overcome it.' But the men who had gone up with him said, 'We are not able to go up against the people, for they are stronger than we.' And they gave the children of Israel a bad report of the land which they had spied out, saying, 'The land through which we have gone as spies is a land that devours its inhabitants, and all the people whom we saw in it are men of great stature. There we saw the giants (the descendants of Anak came from the giants); and we were like grasshoppers in our own sight, and so we were in their sight.'" Numbers 13:30-33

This resulted in a divided people going around in circles for forty years in the wilderness, until God purged them of all unbelief. And although Joshua and Caleb believed the Lord, they too had to go through the same journey. If God had only sent them in, it would have defeated His purpose of a united people possessing their inheritance. The desire of God to have a united people go in and possess the land, was further highlighted by the fact that the Reubenites, the Gadites and half the tribe of Manasseh also had to enter and assist the others in acquiring their inheritance.

Remember, under the reign of Moses they defeated the king of Og and took all the lands east of the Jordan and divided it among the Reubenites, the Gadites and half of the tribe of Manasseh:

"And at that time we took the land from the hand of the two kings of the Amorites who were on this side of the Jordan, from the River Arnon to Mount Hermon (the Sidonians call Hermon Sirion, and the Amorites call it Senir), all the cities of the plain, all Gilead, and all Bashan, as far as Salcah and Edrei, cities of the kingdom of Og in Bashan. For only Og king of Bashan remained of the remnant of the giants. Indeed his bedstead was an iron bedstead. (Is it not in Rabbah of the people of Ammon?) Nine cubits is its length and four cubits its width, according to the standard cubit. "And this land, which we possessed at that time, from Aroer, which is by the River Arnon, and half the mountains of Gilead and its cities, I gave to the Reubenites and the Gadites. The rest of Gilead, and all Bashan, the kingdom of Og, I gave to half the tribe of Manasseh. (All the region of Argob, with all Bashan, was called the land of the giants. Jair the son of Manasseh took all the region of Argob, as far as the border of the Geshurites and the Maachathites, and called

Bashan after his own name, Havoth Jair, to this day.) And I gave Gilead to Machir. And to the Reubenites and the Gadites I gave from Gilead as far as the River Arnon, the middle of the river as the border, as far as the River Jabbok, the border of the people of Ammon; the plain also, with the Jordan as the border, from Chinnereth as far as the east side of the Sea of the Arabah (the Salt Sea), below the slopes of Pisgah. Deuteronomy 3:8-17

However, at that time Moses gave specific instructions concerning their inheritance in relation to the other tribes, which was:

"Then I commanded you at that time saying: 'The Lord your God has given you this land to possess. *All you men of valour shall cross over armed before your brethren,* the children of Israel. 'But your wives, your little ones. And your livestock (I know that you have much livestock) shall stay in your cities which I have given you, *'until the Lord has given rest to your brethren as to you, and they also possess the land which the Lord your God is giving them beyond the Jordan. Then each of you may return to his possession which I have given you.'"* Deuteronomy 3:18-20 (Italics added)

After forty years in the wilderness, during which time God destroyed all the unbelievers and took Moses because of his *disobedience* (not unbelief), God then appointed Joshua as leader of a brand new tribe of people. They were now ready to enter into the land of promise.

It was at that time the command that Moses gave to the Reubenites, the Gadites and half the tribe of Manasseh came into effect, so that a united people went in to possess the land of promise:

"Then Joshua commanded the officers of the people, saying, 'Pass through the camp and command the people, saying, 'Prepare provisions for yourselves, for within three days you will cross over this Jordan, to go in to possess the land which the Lord your God is giving you to possess.' ' *And to the Reubenites, the Gadites, and half the tribe of Manasseh Joshua spoke, saying, 'Remember the word which Moses the servant of the Lord commanded you, saying, 'The Lord your God is giving you rest and is giving you this land.'* 'Your wives, your little ones, and your livestock shall remain in the land which Moses gave you on this side of the Jordan. *But you shall pass before your brethren armed, all your mighty men of valour, and help them, 'until the Lord has given your brethren rest, as He gave you, and they also have taken possession and enjoy it*, which Moses the Lord's servant gave you on this side of the Jordan toward the sunrise.' *So they answered Joshua, saying, 'All that you command us we will do, and wherever you send us we will go.'* " Joshua 1:10-16 (Italics added)

At that stage the Israelites were all united and ready to take the Promised Land. However, unlike the first time when Moses sent the spies and they entered through Hebron in the south, this time they were entering from Jericho in the north. A point worth noting - this time instead of sending out twelve spies, Joshua sends out only two (Joshua 2:1) - representing the power of agreement. By gaining entry into the Promised Land through Jericho, the last place the Israelites were to encounter was *Hebron – The Place of Peace!*

What happened to the Israelites is so relevant to us today. Let us look at some of these principles at work, in the context of present times:

The Church of Jesus Christ today has a destination, a land of promise, to enter into. The Apostle Paul declared it this way:

"And He Himself gave some to be Apostles, some Prophets, some evangelists, and some pastors and teachers, for the equipping of the saints for the work of ministry, for the edifying of the body of Christ, *till we all come into the unity of the faith* and of the knowledge of the Son of God, to a perfect man, to the measure of the stature of the fullness of Christ." Ephesians 4:11-13 (Italics added)

Our land of promise is the fullness of the measure of the stature of Christ and in order to get to that place, unity will be our final frontier. Over the past two thousand years, the Lord has been working to get the Church to a place of maturity. However, there have been several obstacles along the way. We overcame several of them, but the unity of the Church is what the Holy Spirit is working towards, today.

In order for the Church of Jesus Christ to walk in unity, we m*ust* have the full restoration of Apostles and Prophets. Without the full acceptance and restoration of these two ministry gifts, we will not be equipped to enter into this dimension of unity.

However, just as it was in Hebron, where the sons of Anak (giants) dwelt, in the realm of unity some of the biggest devils dwell. So be aware, that the devil will do everything in his power to stop the Church from entering into the place of unity. The Word of God declares in Matthew 18:19:

"Again I say to you that if two of you *agree* on earth concerning anything that they ask, it will be done for them by My Father in heaven." (Italics added)

Agree is a very interesting Greek word, it is the word *sumphoneo*, which is derived from two words: - *sum* = *"together"* and *phoneo* = "to sound". *Sumphoneo* then means – to sound together, to be in accord, to be in harmony or to be united. This is where we get our English word symphony.

God is bringing His Church to the place of *"Hebron"* – a place where we will be a symphony in the earth. This is why Apostles and Prophets are being united in this hour - to join with Evangelists, Pastors and Teachers to equip and unite the church. There is powerful, aggressive prayer going up in every quarter for this final stage to be entered into by the Church, so that the body of Christ can get down to the real issue of doing the work of the ministry.

Networking

Part of the technology that the Lord is using to establish this unity, is *"Networks"*. We are going to see what we call Apostolic and Prophetic networks being established all over the earth. As these are established, individual networks will begin to join and relate to other networks. There will then be "Apostolic Councils" that will be set up for the purpose of discipline and correction. These councils will also be consulted to confirm Apostolic callings and to validate the authenticity and/or accuracy of the doctrines being taught and to also confirm they are in line with the revealed word of God.

The establishment of these *"Networks"* is very important, as they will be used to pioneer much of what the Lord will be doing in these last days.

As with every move of God's Spirit there will be excesses, inaccuracies and outright error. So we can expect to see some networks established for the purpose of drawing people unto themselves, and some for taking control of what the Lord is doing. Others still, will be established to see how many churches, ministries and organization they can have "under" them, and if this happens, we could safely say that these networks will be established and built wrongly, and will eventually collapse. (I recall how recently an "Apostle" contacted me through e-mail and told me that as he visited our website he felt that the Lord wanted me to consider joining his network. I did not know this man, nor heard of him, neither did he know me. Nevertheless he insisted that I join his network and contribute financially to his work. Of course I declined without a second thought, as I am conscious of the fact that erroneous understanding will emerge and for that reason, have to be discerning and wise in this time.)

We have to be very careful of the choices we make when networking. There are some ministries to which God will want us to minister, without entering into an intimate relationship. This is very significant, because as the Prophet Amos declares, "Can two walk together, unless they are agreed?" Amos 3:3

In the book of Isaiah, the Lord reveals to the Prophet the things that are to come. He shows him the eventual state of the end-time church in chapter two, and then goes on to reveal to him the tremendous cleansing that will take place. In the context of this we read the following:

"And in that day seven women shall take hold of one man, saying, 'We will eat our own food and wear our own apparel; Only let us be called by your name, to take away our reproach.'" Isaiah 4:1

I sense that we are now entering into these days, as Apostles and Prophets are being restored. God is now moving in the realm of networks, but I repeat, we have to be careful in networking. As previously stated, there will be some who will establish networks for the wrong reasons. In that event the networks will be built with "seven women" (representing local churches) taking hold of one man (representing an Apostolic/Prophetic network), but without any true representation of the network. They will merely assume the name, without the inner identity and vision of the network. Many of these networks will crumble, as we press further into the true dimension of what God is doing in this hour. Networks that are built on strong relationships and sincerity will survive, even as the purification from the Spirit of God will demand of us in this hour.

Purity, Part Of The Process Towards A Unified Church!

The unity that is to come forth has to be very pure, or else it will not survive. In many places, the people of God are crying out for His Manifested Presence. They are fed-up of programs, activities and shallow religious stuff. Saints from every nation are storming heaven and proclaiming that the *glory of God* must cover the earth, as the waters cover the sea. God is about to respond, but it will be as in the book of Malachi:

"Behold, I send My messenger, and he will prepare the way before Me. *And the Lord, whom you seek, will suddenly come to His temple*, even the Messenger of the covenant, in whom you delight. Behold, He is coming, says the Lord of hosts. '*But who can endure the day of His coming*? And who can stand when He appears? *For He is like a refiner's fire and like launderers' soap*. He will sit as a refiner and a purifier of silver; *He will purify the sons of Levi, and purge them as gold and silver*, that they may offer to the Lord an offering in righteousness." Malachi 3:1-3 (Italics added)

There is a purifying that has already begun in the ranks of professing Christianity.   Some Apostles in training are being cast into the backsides of the desert to be purified.   Others are being purified in motion, they are in charge of networks and ministries, but there is a deep inner work being done.   Still, others are being purified under the *Saul and Laban types of ministries* – Saul took the best from the people and Laban deceived Jacob into working longer for him before receiving his legitimate inheritance.   However, the Father chooses to do it, it is being done, so that the earth can see His Glory through the Church.

When all is said and done the unity that will result will not be superfluous.   It will be real, as invisible threads will connect the body of Christ, and the Church will stand united in the earth. Just as the Internet is invisibly linked and connected, in like manner the Church will be.

Let the trumpet continue to sound loud and clear for all of God's holy Apostles to rise in this hour.   With awesome accuracy and wisdom, let them release the deep truths of God to His Church.   Let there be full acceptance of them as they stand alongside His holy Prophets, Evangelists, Pastors and Teachers to fully equip His people for works of service.   Let all false Apostles be exposed, as the true Apostles rise upon the earth. Selflessness and total commitment to building up the Lord's Body – the Church – will be their operating systems.   Nations will bow before them, as they proclaim a mighty Jesus and cause the glory of God to be seen.

Rise up Apostles, and stand in unity with the other equippers, as an example to the Body of Christ that unity is possible.   Let there be networking from town to town, from country to country, from nation to nation, from region to region, from continent to continent until the earth is covered with the knowledge of the glory of the Lord as the waters cover the sea.

Rise up Apostles and take your place in the Church's finest hour, as we begin to see a mature, united Church take shape in the earth. This is the hour to make the prayer of Jesus in John 17 a living reality. This is the hour to declare, "this is that, which was spoke by the Apostle and High Priest of our confession, Christ Jesus."

Appendix
Questions and Answers

In the following we will deal with questions commonly asked about Apostles and Apostolic Ministry.

Q: The Bible declares that the foundation of the Church was laid upon the Apostles and Prophets, with Jesus Christ, Himself being the Chief Cornerstone. So why do we now need the ministry of the Apostle restored?

A: In answering this question, Let us go back to Matthew 16:13-18

"When Jesus came into the region of Caesarea Philippi, He asked His disciples, saying, 'Who do men say that I, the Son of Man, am?' So they said, 'Some say John the Baptist, some say Elijah, and others Jeremiah or one of the Prophets.' He said to them, 'But who do you say that I am?' Simon Peter answered and said, 'You are the Christ, the Son of the living God.' Jesus answered and said to him, 'Blessed are you, Simon Bar-Jonah, for flesh and blood has not *revealed* this to you, but My Father who is in heaven. And I also say to you that you are Peter, *and on this rock I will build My church*, and the gates of Hades shall not prevail against it." (Italics added)

On what was Jesus going to build His Church? Was it on Peter or on the revelation that He, Jesus, was the Son of God?

It was on the revelation that Peter had. Remember the issue here was "who do you say that I am?" And it was the revelation that Peter got that released the awesome truth that Jesus declared:

"Blessed are you, Simon Bar-Jonah, for flesh and blood has not revealed this to you, but My Father who is in heaven. And I also say to you that you are Peter, and on this rock I will build My church, and the gates of Hades shall not prevail against it"

And I also say to you that you are Peter (which is the Greek word *Petros*, and means *little rock*, or *piece of rock*) and on this rock (which is the Greek word *Petra and means a mass of rock, or a huge rock*) I will build My Church.

In like manner, the Church is being built upon the foundation of Apostles and Prophets - (in essence it is being built upon the revelation of Christ that is released through the Apostolic and Prophetic ministry gifts) with Jesus Christ, Himself being the cornerstone – the stone from which everything is connected.

You will agree with me that the Church is not yet finished, and because of this there is a definite need for the ministry gift of the Apostle. There is a definite anointing upon Apostles and Prophets to bring clarity to the word of God. In every generation we need that clarity, or we will loose sight of the true Church.

The reason why we have so much of erroneous teachings and "*spooky*" things in the name of Christianity is because the ministry of the Apostle was lost. As the end draws closer upon us, there must be a full restoration of Apostles, so that the Church can remain accurate and strong for the soon return of our King.

Q: If the Church is built upon the revelation that Apostles bring, are we to see new doctrines being introduced into the Church?

A: No! And I want to emphatically state NO. All the doctrine that the Church will ever need to be built upon accurately has already been given. However, having said that, part of the Apostolic equipment is to bring clearer revelation of doctrine and correct interpretation of scripture.

There are hidden or sealed mysteries that God by His Spirit has put into the scriptures, and they can only be known by revelation. This is part of the grace that has been released to the Apostles, to decode and unlock these mysteries to the Church. The Apostle Paul in writing to the Corinthian church declared:

"And I, brethren, when I came to you, did not come with excellence of speech or of wisdom declaring to you the testimony of God. For I determined not to know anything among you except Jesus Christ and Him crucified. I was with you in weakness, in fear, and in much trembling. And my speech and my preaching were not with persuasive words of human wisdom, but in demonstration of the Spirit and of power, that your faith should not be in the wisdom of men but in the power of God. However, we speak wisdom among those who are mature, yet not the wisdom of this age, nor of the rulers of this age, who are coming to nothing. But *we speak the wisdom of God in a mystery, the hidden wisdom* which God ordained before the ages for our glory, which none of the rulers of this age knew; for had they known, they would not have crucified the Lord of glory. But as it is written– *'Eye has*

*not seen, nor ear heard, nor have entered into the heart
of man The things which God has prepared for those who
love Him' But God has revealed them to us through His
Spirit. For the Spirit searches all things, yes, the deep
things of God."* 1 Corinthians 2:1-10 (Italics added)

What the Apostle Paul was actually saying is, that part of
the Apostolic grace is the divine ability to receive from God
through the Holy Spirit, the understanding of the mysteries that
He hid.

In speaking to His Apostles, Jesus declared this same truth
to them. In the gospel of Matthew, Jesus had just finished
teaching the parable of the sower and the seed and concluded
His sermon by telling the multitude: "He who has ears to hear,
let him hear!" Matthew 13:9. He then takes His Apostles (in
training) aside and declares this powerful truth to them:

"And the disciples came and said to Him, 'Why do You
speak to them in parables?' He answered and said to
them, 'Because *it has been given to you to know the
mysteries of the kingdom of heaven*, but to them it has not
been given.' " Matthew 13:10-11 (Italics added)

Again we see this word *mystery* appearing.

Mystery: Is the Greek word *musterion* and it comes from the
root word *mueo*, which means, "to initiate into mysteries,"
hence a secret known only to the initiated, something hidden,
requiring special revelation.

This word *musterion* that is used here in the New Testament
denotes something that people could never know by their own
understanding, but demands a revelation from God.

This knowledge of the mysteries of the kingdom of heaven is given to every believer. However, God uses the Apostolic grace to unlock them to His Church.

Another passage of scripture that clarifies this is:

"I now rejoice in my sufferings for you, and fill up in my flesh what is lacking in the afflictions of Christ, for the sake of His body, which is the church, of which I became a minister according to the stewardship from God which was given to me for you, to fulfill the word of God, *the mystery* which has been hidden from ages and from generations, but now has been revealed to his saints. To them God willed to make known what are the riches of the glory of *this mystery* among the Gentiles: which is Christ in you, the hope of glory. Him we preach, warning every man and teaching every man in all wisdom, that we may present every man perfect in Christ Jesus. To this end I also labour, striving according to His working which works in me mightily." Colossians 1:24-29 (Italics added)

So, Apostles are not to introduce any "*new*" doctrine to the Church, but they are to uncover truths already established in the Word of God.

In the Apostle John's letter we read of a remarkable scenario:

"And I saw in the right hand of Him who sat on the throne a scroll written inside and on the back, sealed with seven seals. Then I saw a strong angel proclaiming with a loud voice, 'Who is worthy to open the scroll and to loose its seals?' And no one in heaven or on the earth or under the earth was able to open the scroll, or to look at it. So I wept much, because no one was found worthy to open and read the scroll, or to look at it. But one of the elders said to me, 'Do not weep. Behold, the Lion of the tribe of Judah, the Root of David, has prevailed to open the scroll and to loose its seven seals.' And I looked, and behold, in the midst of the throne and of the four living creatures, and in the midst of the elders, stood a Lamb as though it had been slain. Having seven horns and seven eyes, which are the seven Spirits of God sent into all the earth. Then He came and took the scroll out of the right hand of Him who sat on the throne. Revelation 5:1-7

This portion of scripture speaks of certain events that are to take place, and only Jesus is able to open and read these events. Most of what the Apostle John saw, was sealed up for this end-time, and will be revealed by God through His holy Apostles and Prophets.

The revelation will not be extra-biblical, but solely based on the pure and unadulterated word of God.

Q: Are there different types of Apostles?

A: Yes, the bible describes several types of Apostles. Here are a few:

♦ We had James, the brother of our Lord and Saviour Jesus Christ, who was the presiding Apostle of the Jerusalem church. It would seem that the only church James was ever involved in planting, was the Jerusalem church. He never traveled. Did very little in miracles, signs and wonders. Did not write much, apart from the book that bears his name in the New Testament. His Apostolic function was mainly to bring judgement on those who called themselves Apostles, and to bring divine clarity on matters involving the operation of the church.

♦ We had Barnabas, who was a tremendous relationship builder. He was the one who introduced the Apostle Paul (ex church destroyer Saul) to the church. He never wrote any books. However, he was a trainer of men and functioned as a mentor.

♦ We had Peter, who was an Apostle to the Jews.

♦ We also had Paul who primarily was an apostle to the Gentiles. He wrote books, traveled extensively, planted new churches mentored and fathered and flowed constantly in miracles, signs and wonders.

These are just a few of the different types of Apostles in the scriptures.

Q: Are Missionaries and Apostles the same?

A: Not necessarily. In today's understanding a missionary is one who is sent to a foreign land with a message from God, and in most cases to establish a new church plant. When that message is delivered then the calling ceases. So really a missionary is considered to be a temporary Apostle. However, with an Apostle that has been anointed and appointed by the Lord, this designation is permanent and most times involves much more than new churches being planted.

Q: What are some of the identifiable characteristics of Apostles and Apostolic ministry?

A: There are several identifiable characteristics of Apostles and Apostolic ministry; however, I will confine this list to a few.

- They are church planters.

- They are foundational ministries.

- They are pioneers and do not build upon another's foundation.

- They have a very strong anointing for breakthrough.

- They move in miracles, signs and wonders.

- They move in revelation.

- They father and mentor others.

- They have a very strong ministry in prayer and the ministry of the word of God.

- Apostolic ministries move very strong in warfare.

- They are able to impart spiritual gifts.

- They demonstrate a very high capacity to care for other churches.

- They are ministry equippers.

- They are able to bring ministries and ministers together.

Q: Are Apostles the highest authority in the Church?

A: *No!* The highest authority in the Church remains Jesus Christ and His revealed word.

Q: Who then, are Apostles accountable to?

A: This is a very sensitive issue, and must be dealt with in three distinct areas. First, we need to understand that apostles are not a law unto themselves. Ergo - the first area that is very evident is that of accountability to the Lord and His word. We must be very clear that the Lord is the one who is in charge of His Church, and can bring correction and judgment as He sees fit.

The second area of accountability for Apostles, is fellow Apostles and Church leaders. The word of God encourages us to be submitted one to another and this works in the area of leadership too. Some may say, "my Apostleship is not of man but of God, hence the reason I do not need to submit to any man". In response to that, we will do well to heed the example set by the noted Apostle Paul, (who was used by the Lord to do more for the New Testament Church than most of us will ever do). Even though he was called and ordained by the Lord Himself, the apostle Paul found it necessary to go to Jerusalem and submit to the Apostolic Council headed by James (Acts 15:1-35).

The third area of accountability for Apostles is to their local church, and to churches that they are sent to. This area is one that can really show the heart of true and false Apostles.

Other Titles By The Author

Apostolic Purity
In Pursuit of His Excellence
A Sequel to Five Pillars of The Apostolic

In every dispensation, in every move of God's Holy Spirit to bring restoration and reformation to His Church, righteousness, holiness and purity has always been of utmost importance to the Lord. And it is no different in the current move of God that is bringing apostolic restoration to His Church. In many places, the people of God are crying out for His Manifested Presence. Fed-up with mere programs, activities and shallow religious works, saints from every nation are storming heaven and proclaiming that the *Glory of God* must cover the earth, as the waters cover the sea.

There is a purifying that has already begun in the ranks of professing Christianity. Some apostles in training are being cast into the backsides of the desert to be purified. Others are being purified in motion, they are in charge of networks and ministries, but there is a deep inner work being done. Still, others are being purified under the *Saul and Laban types of ministries* – Saul took the best from the people and Laban deceived Jacob into working longer for him before receiving his legitimate inheritance. However, the Father chooses to do it, it is being done, so that the earth can see His Glory through the Church.

Kingdom Advancing Prayer
Volumes I & II

Part of the technology that is being released into the Church as the Lord restores Apostles, is what we describe as Kingdom Advancing Prayer. This kind of prayer puts the Kingdom of God first and foremost; it is above any personal need or agenda. It is similar to the kind of prayer that Elijah prayed, as the Lord used him to turn a whole nation around, and destroy the demonic influence that threatened to thwart the Lord's purpose. It is reflective of the prayer that Jesus prayed as He prepared to bring to completion His Father's will and go to the cross.

The Church of Jesus Christ is stronger and much more determined and equipped than she has ever been, and strong, aggressive, powerful, Spirit-Filled, Kingdom-centred prayers are being lifted in every nation in the earth. We are seeing the emergence of Houses of Prayer all over the earth with prayer going up 24/7. Prayer is calling for the Bridegroom's return, and for the Bride to be made ready. Prayers that are storming the heavens and binding the *"strong men"*, declaring and decreeing God's Kingdom rule in every jurisdiction. This is what we call Kingdom Advancing Prayer. This kind of prayer is released from the heart of Father God into the hearts of His people, as we seek for His Glory to cover the earth as the waters cover the sea. What a *Glorious Day* to be *alive* and to be in the *Will and Plan of Father God! Hallelujah!*

To Order Contact:
Word Alive Press Inc.
131 Cordite Road · Winnipeg, MB, R3W 1S1 · Canada
Phone: 866·967·3782 · Fax: 800·352·9272

Identifying And Defeating The Jezebel Spirit

I declare to you with the greatest of conviction that we are living in the days when Malachi 4:5-6 is being fulfilled. The Elijah spirit is truly in the earth as the Lord prepares His Church for the return of Jesus and the culmination of all things. However, as it was in the days of Elijah of old so it is in these days.

Elijah in his day had to confront and deal with a false spiritual order and government that was established and set up by an evil woman called Jezebel and her spineless husband called Ahab. This spirit is still active in the earth and in the Church; however the Lord is restoring His holy apostles and prophets to identify and destroy this spirit as recorded in Revelation 2:18-23

As you read through the pages of this book it is my prayer that you will be enlightened to the reality of the battle and the strategy the Lord has given us to effect the ultimate victory.

To Order Contact:
Dominion-Life International
Box 44592 Garden Park
Vancouver, BC, V5M 4R8, Canada
Phone: 604·953·1087 · Fax: 604·953·1085
Or visit our website at http://www.dominion-life.org

Other Titles Recommended By The Author

Authored By Dr. **Kelley Varner**

Moses, The Master And The Manchild	ISBN 0-7684-2121-7
The Three Prejudices	ISBN 1-56043-187-3
The More Excellent Ministry	ISBN 0-914903-60-8
The Priesthood Is Changing	ISBN 1-56043-033-8
Prevail	ISND 0-938612-06-9

To Order Contact Destiny Image
P.O. Box 310, Shippensburg, PA 17257-0310
Or on the Internet at
www.reapernet.com

Authored By **Apostle John Eckhardt**

Moving In The Apostolic	ISBN 0-8307-2373-0
The Ministry Anointing Of The Apostle	ISBN 0-9630567-6-X
Leadershift – Transitioning From The Pastoral To The Apostolic	ISBN 1-883927-14-5
Presbyteries And Apostolic Teams	ISBN 1-883927-13-7
Proton Believers	ISBN 1-883927-15-3
50 Truths Concerning Apostolic Ministry	ISBN 1-883927-04-8

To Order Contact Crusaders I.M.P.A.C.T
P.O. Box 492, Matteson, IL 60443
708·922·0983
www.impactnetwork.net

Authored By **Dr. Jonathan David**

Apostolic Strategies Affecting Nations

Proclaiming Liberty To The Captives

Developing A Prophetic Ministry

Business Sense For Making Dollars

Jesus, God's Greatest Move

To Order Contact Crusaders I.M.P.A.C.T
P.O. Box 492, Matteson, IL 60443
708·922·0983
www.impactnetwork.net

OR

Dr. Jonathan David
No: 4, Taman Mas Ria, Jalan Junid,
84000 Muar, Jahor Malaysia
Tel: (06)·9534066 Fax: (06)·9531031
www.jonathan-david.org

Authored By **Dr. Noel Woodroffe**

The Present Reformation	ISBN 976-8115-03-3
The Prophetic Dimension	ISBN 976-8115-05-X
Spiritual Government	ISBN 976-8115-00-9
The Ultimate Warrior	ISBN 976-8115-01-7

To Order Contact Elijah Centre
P.O. Bag 317
Tunapuna, Trinidad, W.I
Phone 868·662·5673
www.elijahcentre.org

Authored By **Dr. Roger Sapp**

The Last Apostles On Earth ISBN 1-56043-568-2

Apostolic Fathers And ISBN 0-9662085-4-4
Spiritual Bastards

Performing Miracles And Healing ISBN 0-9662085-5-2

To Order Contact All Nations Ministry
P.O. Box 92847, Southlake, TX 76092
817-514-0653
www.allnationsmin.org

Authored By **Pastor Jana Alcorn**

The Ministry Of Excellence

Prophetic Encounters--Facilitating Change Through The Voice Of
The Spirit

To Order Contact Harvest Church
700 Motley Street - PO Box 205
Albertville, Alabama 35950
Phone 256-891-1650
www.MinistryOfExcellence.com

CPSIA information can be obtained at www.ICGtesting.com
Printed in the USA
LVOW060332280512

283525LV00001B/102/A